CONQUERING FEAR

SUPER INCREDIBLE FAITH DEVOTIONAL

Julia Ball

Conquering Fear 52 Week Devotional! Ages 10-12

RoseKidz® is an imprint of
Rose Publishing, LLC
P.O. Box 3473
Peabody, Massachusetts 01961-3473 USA
www.hendricksonrose.com

Cover and Interior Design: Drew McCall

ISBN: 978-1-62862-782-4
RoseKidz® reorder #L50021
JUVENILE NONFICTION/Religious/Christian/Devotional & Prayer

Printed in the United States of America
Printed April 2019

CONTENTS

CONTENTS

WEEK 1
DAY 1

WHO IS JESUS?

Read This!

> *Jesus Christ is the same yesterday, today, and forever.*
>
> Hebrews 13:8

Can you imagine living to be 100 years old? That would be a lot of candles on your birthday cake. If you were 100 years old, it would seem like you had been alive practically forever.

You could do a lot of things in 100 years—travel the world, have a giant family, and eat a lot of delicious food! Think about all the places you would see and all the people you would know! One hundred years is a lot of time to fill.

Even though 100 seems really old to us, there is someone who is even older than that. That someone is Jesus. In fact, he doesn't have an age at all.

Jesus has existed forever, and the Bible tells us that he has no beginning and no end. Before the world existed, he was in Heaven with God. Before you were born, he was in Heaven with God. And for as far into the future as you can imagine, he will be there, looking out for the world.

Wow! That is certainly incredible. The fact that Jesus has always existed tells us that he is not just an ordinary person. An ordinary person couldn't exist forever. But Jesus can, and he does! That makes him special. In fact, it makes him God.

Fear Buster

Jesus has always been in your life. And, there will never be a time in your life that Jesus won't be there. Even when times are hard, scary, or confusing, you can trust that Jesus will be by your side!

Try This!

A lot of cool things have been invented in history. Jesus has been there to see them all. Underneath these pictures of cool inventions, write what you imagine God and Jesus might say about them!

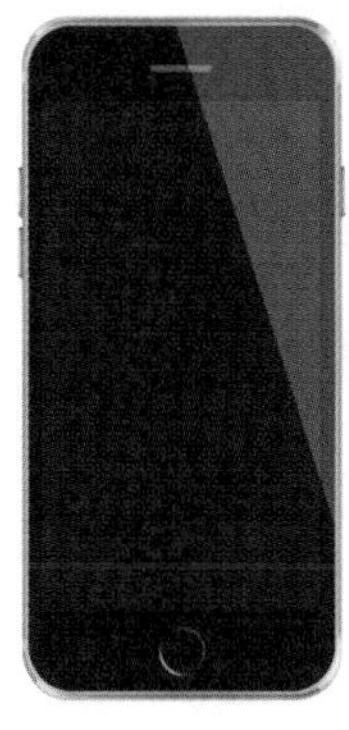

WHO IS JESUS?

Try This!

Earlier this week, we talked about being 100 years old. Imagine what life was like for kids 100 years ago. On these stick figures, draw what you imagine these kids' faces, clothes, and maybe even toys or a house would have looked like. Jesus was with them, just like he is with you.

WHO IS JESUS?

WEEK 1
DAY 4

Read This!

A voice from Heaven said, "This is my dearly loved Son, who brings me great joy."

Matthew 3:17

Timothy was so excited when he hit a home run at his little league game! His face beamed with pride as he raced around the bases and arrived back at home plate.

He could see the smiles on his teammates' faces as he walked back to the bench. His coach gave him a huge high-five, and his best buddy, Jack, gave him a big hug. He felt awesome!

All of a sudden, he saw his dad in the crowd yelling, "Yeah, Timmy! That's my boy! That's my son!" at the top of his lungs. He was cheering and clapping and jumping! It might have been a little embarrassing, but Timothy still thought it was pretty cool. His dad was proud of him, and he wanted everyone to know that he was his son.

Timothy's dad made sure everyone at the game knew that his son just got a home run. He was so proud! When Jesus was on Earth, his heavenly Father wanted everyone to know who he was. When Jesus was baptized on Earth, God's voice boomed from the Heavens, telling everyone that this was his Son! He was proud of him, and wanted everyone to know.

Jesus is God's Son! That means he is more than just a regular guy. He is God himself. He is part of God, along with the Father and the Holy Spirit. This means he isn't just a nice teacher or a good man but someone who needs to be obeyed and worshiped. God made clear that Jesus is his Son, and he wants us to know and follow him!

Prayer Prompt

Aren't you glad that God tells us all we need to know about him? Thank him for telling us that Jesus is his Son, and ask him to show you more about him.

WEEK 1
DAY 5

WHO IS JESUS?

Try This!

Write a letter that you think God would have sent from Heaven to Jesus on Earth. What would he say? What do you think he would have wanted people to know?

WHO IS JESUS?

WEEK 1
DAY 6

Try This!

Draw a poster or collage of things you know about Jesus and things you would like to learn about him in this book. Use superhero words, pictures, and drawings to make your poster.

WEEK 2
DAY 1

JESUS CAME TO EARTH

Read This!

"Let's go to Bethlehem! Let's see this thing that has happened, which the Lord has told us about."

Luke 2:15

Superheroes are amazing. Not only do they have cool outfits and capes, but every superhero has their own special mission. When people need help, superheroes come to the rescue! They fight against bad guys! They save the day!

Jesus, the ultimate superhero, was given the greatest rescue mission of all time—to come to Earth and save us! He didn't fly in as a superhero with a cool cape though. He came in a way that nobody expected. Jesus came to a town called Bethlehem as a tiny baby in a manger.

Imagine that! Jesus decided to leave Heaven and become a baby. He didn't have an amazing entrance into the world. It was quiet and ordinary. Even though the way he came was ordinary, it was still amazing! Jesus left his power and home in Heaven to come to Earth so he could rescue you and me. That sounds like something a superhero would do!

Fear Buster

Jesus came to Earth so he could know people just like you. When you are scared, you can think about the fact that Jesus wants to be close to you! No need to fear when Jesus is near!

JESUS CAME TO EARTH

WEEK 2
DAY 2

Try This!

This is a newspaper from Bethlehem on the day Jesus was born. Below, draw some pictures of the important event. If you can, write a headline to go along with it. This news changed the world forever!

Current Press

BETHLEHEM BEE

All news in one newspaper

Issue: 240460

WEEK 2 DAY 3

JESUS CAME TO EARTH

Try This!

Angels, like the one on this page, made an amazing announcement when Jesus was born. They sang a song from the Heavens. Use your imagination and make up a song, poem, or dance about Jesus' birth. You can write it down here and then perform it for your family. Celebrate Jesus' birth!

JESUS CAME TO EARTH

WEEK 2
DAY 4

She will have a son, and you are to name him Jesus, for he will save his people from their sins.

Matthew 1:21

Read This!

Laura and Liam were so excited for Friday! They had been working hard for the past month to plan a special surprise for their mom's birthday. With their dad's help, they baked a delicious chocolate cake. Liam had made some awesome decorations, and Laura had made a beautiful card. It seemed like they had been planning this surprise forever, and now the day was almost here.

Just like Laura and Liam were planning a special day for their mom, God planned Jesus' special arrival to Earth as a baby. God spent a lot longer than a month planning Jesus' arrival. He had been planning it since the beginning of time! God knew that people would need someone to save them from the messy world they lived in and the bad things they had done. He knew they needed more than a superhero. They needed a Savior.

That's why he planned for Jesus to come! It wasn't a surprise or a mistake. It was part of God's amazing plan from the beginning. God's plan for Jesus was perfect. It makes a way for us to know him!

Prayer Prompt

Praise God for his amazing plan of sending Jesus and his amazing plan for you!

JESUS CAME TO EARTH

Try This!

This maze shows Jesus leaving Heaven and coming to Earth! After you've completed the maze, take a minute to thank God for sending Jesus from Heaven.

Answers on Page 318

JESUS CAME TO EARTH

WEEK 2
DAY 6

Try This!

Decipher the code to figure out God's special plan for sending Jesus! Each number represents a letter of the alphabet. Hint: this puzzle is as easy as ABC, 123! Look up Matthew 1:21 if you need help.

Answers on Page 318

WEEK 3
DAY 1

JESUS DID AMAZING THINGS

> *Jesus traveled through all the towns and villages of that area, teaching in the synagogues and announcing the Good News about the kingdom. And he healed every kind of disease and illness.*
>
> Matthew 9:35

Read This!

Anna was sick, and she was tired. For the past twelve years, she had dealt with this horrible illness. Nobody was sure what it was, and nobody seemed to know what caused it. It was a mystery to everyone—the priests, the doctors, and especially to her. She had spent all her money on doctors and medicines, but her sickness just kept getting worse.

One day, she heard about a special man named Jesus who was coming to town. People said he did amazing things like heal sick people and raise the dead! She had to meet him. So, on the day he passed through town, she pushed her way through the crowd and stumbled into Jesus. She couldn't get his attention, so she just grabbed his coat. *Bam!* Instantly, she was better. All her sickness was gone.

Who was this man? He had power like she had never experienced. As she began to tell people about her miracle, she learned this wasn't the only miracle he had performed. He had made a blind man see, a paralyzed man walk, and a dead little girl come back to life. People were whispering, "Maybe he isn't just a man. Maybe he's God!" Could it be true?

Fear Buster

Being sick, or knowing someone who is, can be really scary. Jesus is able to heal the sick and be close to us when we are hurt! When you're sick, pray to Jesus, the God of miracles.

JESUS DID AMAZING THINGS

WEEK 3
DAY 2

Try This!

Anna's story is found in Matthew 9:20–22. We don't actually know her name, but we do know her story. Find it in your Bible, and draw a comic strip illustrating the events of Anna's story in the spaces below.

JESUS DID AMAZING THINGS

Try This!

Jesus' miracles showed that his power is greater than any superhero's! Design a superhero logo that you think would represent Jesus.

JESUS DID AMAZING THINGS

WEEK 3
DAY 4

About three o'clock in the morning, Jesus came toward them, walking on the water.

Matthew 14:25

Read This!

Have you ever experienced a terrible storm? Maybe it was a blizzard, a hurricane, or just a lot of rain. Storms can be scary on land, but can you imagine how much scarier they would be if you were on a boat?

That is exactly what happened to Jesus' disciples! They were crossing the sea on a boat when all of a sudden, a storm struck. The wind was blowing and the waves were beating on the boat. It must have been terrifying! If that wasn't scary enough, they saw someone walking toward them on the water.

Was it a ghost? A dream? Who could walk on water? They were shocked to see that it was Jesus walking toward them on the waves. Even though it was stormy all around them, he walked right up to the boat! He even stopped the storm!

What kind of person was Jesus? He walked on water! The winds and waves stopped when he spoke! Wow! Only God could do miracles like this one. Seeing Jesus perform this amazing feat grew the disciples' faith. They knew they could trust and follow Jesus. He could do anything. When we read these stories, we can know that we can trust and follow him too!

Prayer Prompt

Have you ever faced a "storm" in your life? Something hard or scary? Pray and ask God to help you trust Jesus when you face hard times or "storms."

Try This!

Grab some blue food coloring, scissors, tape, and cardstock or other materials you have lying around.

Get your creative juices flowing and try to recreate the scene from this story in Matthew 14. Use some water in a dish or sink and add a few drops of blue food coloring. You have your stormy sea!

Now, create a boat using cardstock, scissors, tape or any other materials you can find! Act out the story of Jesus, the disciples, and the storm!

Try This!

Draw Jesus walking on the water in this picture of the stormy sea. What do you think the disciples' faces looked like? Draw a boat, and add them in, too!

WEEK 4 DAY 1

JESUS DIED FOR US

> *The Son of Man must . . . be crucified, and that he would rise again on the third day.*
> Luke 24:7

Read This!

Sometimes, Kara wished she could know what would happen in the future. She wondered what the weather would be like next week for her birthday. Would it be snowing or raining? She wished she could know how tall she would be in sixth grade. Would she be tall enough to try out for the basketball team? And she really wished she knew what she would be when she got older. Would she be a doctor, a carpenter, or a teacher?

The future was scary and exciting, and she wished she could know it all now!

All of us have wished we could know what would happen in the future. There is really only one person who has ever lived who knew the future, and that person was Jesus. He knew exactly what would happen in his future, and it was scary! Jesus knew that he was going to die on a cross.

While he lived on Earth, Jesus told his disciples many times that he was going to die on a cross. This was his big mission on Earth. While his disciples didn't understand why he had to die, and could hardly believe this was true, Jesus knew he had to die. It was all a part of God's incredible plan for him and for us!

Fear Buster

Thank God that he knows the future! Although thinking about the future can be both scary and exciting, we can know that Jesus knows everything that will happen. We don't have to be scared when the future is in his hands!

JESUS DIED FOR US

WEEK 4
DAY 2

Try This!

Jesus had the power to know the future, not because he was magical, but because he was God. What are some of the things you wish you knew about your future? Make a list of them on this page, and say a prayer trusting Jesus with them.

Week 4 Day 3

Jesus Died for Us

Try This!

Draw what you think the disciples would have looked like when they found out Jesus was going to die. As you draw and color, imagine how they would have felt when this happened. What were their faces like? Try to draw their expressions.

JESUS DIED FOR US

WEEK 4
DAY 4

When Jesus had tasted it, he said, "It is finished!" Then he bowed his head and gave up his spirit.

John 19:30

Read This!

Peter was one of Jesus' best friends. He had been with Jesus for three years, following him everywhere he went. He wished that he didn't have to follow Jesus here though, to a hill called Golgotha. This hill is where they took criminals to die on crosses. Jesus wasn't a criminal, but they nailed him to a cross and left him to die.

Peter couldn't understand why Jesus had to die. It seemed confusing, sad, and unfair. How could this be part of God's plan? Jesus was supposed to save them all!

What Peter didn't understand was that by dying on the cross, Jesus was saving us. By dying on the cross, Jesus did what nobody else could do: fix our relationship with God. He became a sacrifice for our sins that day.

A sacrifice is when you give up something important for something more important. Jesus gave up his life for us. Dying on the cross was how he showed his love for us. It was the most super incredible thing he could ever do.

Prayer Prompt

Give thanks to Jesus for dying on the cross for you.

WEEK 4
DAY 5

JESUS DIED FOR US

Try This!

Use the letters of the word "CROSS" and make an acrostic poem (one line for each letter) describing what happened to Jesus on the cross. Look up John 19 in your Bible if you need some help!

C ______________________________

R ______________________________

O ______________________________

S ______________________________

S ______________________________

JESUS DIED FOR US

WEEK 4
DAY 6

Try This!

It's important for us to remember what Jesus did for us on the cross. There are lots of ways to remember things, but one way is to use sticky notes. Make a sticky note with a picture or sentence reminding you of something important about Jesus dying on the cross. Stick it in your room or on your mirror to remember what Jesus did for you this week! Practice what you'll write on the sticky note below!

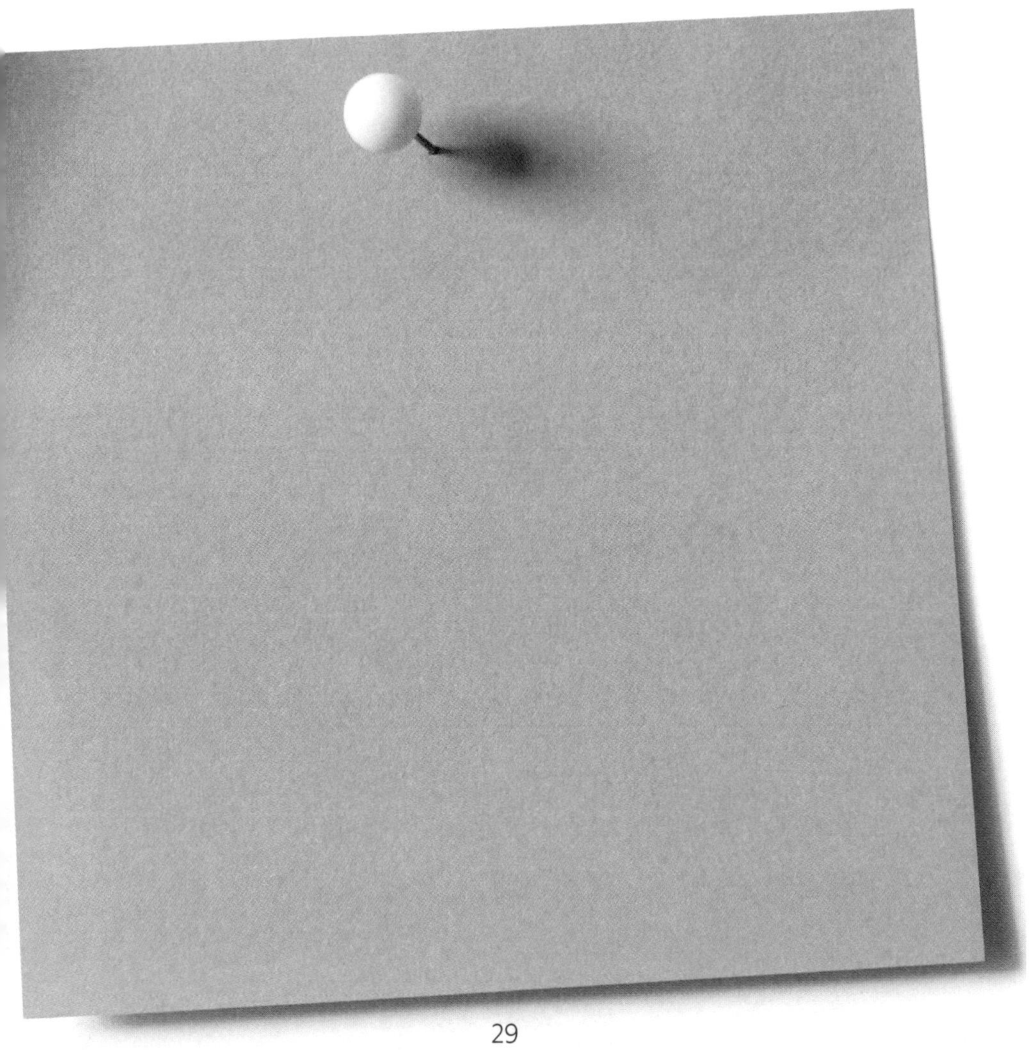

WEEK 5
DAY 1

JESUS IS ALIVE

> *Why are you looking among the dead for someone who is alive? He isn't here! He is risen from the dead!*
> Luke 24:5-6

Read This!

Mary, one of Jesus' closest friends, got up early on Sunday morning to head to the cave where they had buried Jesus. She and her friends wanted to say their goodbyes to Jesus and bring perfumes and spices as a final gift.

Mary and the other women couldn't believe their eyes when they arrived at the cave. The boulder at its front was rolled away, and there were angels standing there! These angels proclaimed unbelievable news. Jesus was no longer dead, he was alive!

These women raced to share the news with their friends, and before long, they saw Jesus! He was definitely alive. God kept his promise to them. While Jesus had to die as a sacrifice, he had been raised from the dead. This showed everyone how powerful God was!

A sad story has a beautiful, exciting ending. There is nothing that God cannot do. Because of his power, Jesus is alive!

Fear Buster

Our incredible God is powerful! He is powerful enough to raise someone from the dead. Knowing his power can help us face any scary situation. We serve an amazing God.

JESUS IS ALIVE

WEEK 5
DAY 2

Try This!

Imagine how excited Jesus' disciples must have been when they found out Jesus was alive! After they got over the shock, I am sure they celebrated. Play some of your favorite Christian music, turn it up loud, and have a dance party (by yourself, with a friend, or family member) to celebrate Jesus being alive. Write down some words in the space below that remind you of celebrating!

Try This!

When the disciples found out Jesus was alive, they wanted to share the good news with everyone they could! Make a card or poster sharing the news that Jesus is alive. You can write or draw on it, or maybe even include an invitation to your church. Give it to a friend to let them know that Jesus is alive!

JESUS IS ALIVE

WEEK 5
DAY 4

When he had cleansed us from our sins, he sat down in the place of honor at the right hand of the majestic God in Heaven.

Hebrews 1:3

Read This!

Alisha really missed her best friend, Jake, after he moved across the country. She missed hanging out after school, sitting in Sunday school together at church, and eating lunch together in the cafeteria. Why did he have to be so far away?

Even though they were separated, Alisha knew Jake was still her friend. Her mom let her borrow her phone once a week so she could video-chat with Jake and his mom. She had even sent Jake a letter in the mail, and he sent one back. Even though she couldn't see Jake every day, she knew they were still best friends.

When Jesus left Earth, his friends knew they would miss him. They had spent every day together for three years, and he had just been raised from the dead! They wished they could spend the rest of their lives with him, but they knew he had to return to Heaven with God. While he was in Heaven, he would be ruling with power, talking to God on their behalf, and giving them strength to follow him. They would know he was still there, even if they couldn't see him.

Today, Jesus is still in Heaven with God! Even though he's no longer on Earth, we can know that he's with us, helping us every day!

Prayer Prompt

Spend a few minutes talking to God in Heaven, thanking him that you can know Jesus, even if you can't see him.

JESUS IS ALIVE

Try This!

Jesus returned to Heaven on the clouds. You can read about it in Acts 1. What do you think Heaven looked like when Jesus returned to it? Use your imagination, and draw a picture of what you think it may look like!

Try This!

The Bible says that Jesus sits in Heaven, next to God the Father's throne! While he's there, he is talking to God on our behalf! On the picture of this throne, write down the things you would like God to know about you. They can be secrets or special needs you have in your life.

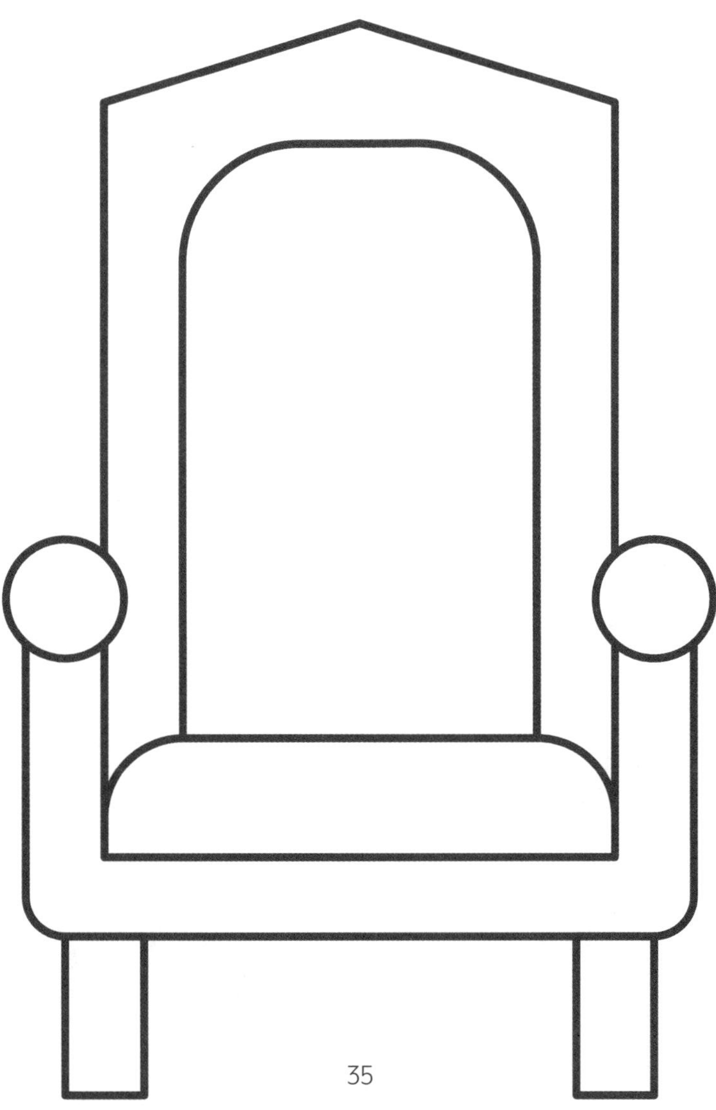

WEEK 6
DAY 1

WE NEED FAITH TO FOLLOW JESUS

> *For this is how God loved the world: He gave his one and only Son, so that everyone who believes in him will not perish but have eternal life.*
>
> John 3:16

Read This!

Alexa and her dad sat on her bed one night, talking before she went to sleep. As they chatted, Alexa suddenly thought of a question, and blurted it out quickly.

"Dad, what does it mean to have faith? I hear the pastor and my children's church teacher talk about it all the time, but what does that word even mean?"

Her dad smiled and leaned in a little closer. "*Faith* means to trust in something completely," he explained. "No matter what other people say or do, having faith means believing that God is real and that Jesus did what the Bible says he did, that he lived, died, and rose again.

Alexa sighed, "Dad, that sounds hard! It's hard to trust in someone you can't even see."

"I know!" Her dad replied. "But, the cool part about having faith is that when we trust God, he gives us more faith! Believing in him is just the start of the journey. He helps us along the rest of the way."

Alexa smiled, and her eyes started to get heavy. "That makes sense, Dad. I want to have faith in Jesus! 3I believe he can help me."

Fear Buster

Faith means trusting in God all the time. Faith helps us fight when we are scared. Even when we can't see God, we can trust him in every situation!

WE NEED FAITH TO FOLLOW JESUS

WEEK 6
DAY 2

Try This!

Have you ever done a trust fall before? A trust fall is when you stand in front of a friend, and then fall backwards, trusting that they'll catch you. Doing a trust fall takes having faith in the person behind you, even if you can't see. Find a friend to do some trust falls with today, and as you do, think about what it's like having faith in God, who you can't see. Talk about it together. Then, write some of your thoughts about trusting God below.

WEEK 6
DAY 3

WE NEED FAITH TO FOLLOW JESUS

Try This!

Sometimes it's hard to have faith in Jesus because we can't physically see him anymore. Do this experiment with a grown-up to show how seeing is not believing.

Materials:

- 1 package of yeast
- ¼ cup of warm water
- 1 teaspoon sugar

Directions:

1. Mix the yeast, water, and sugar together.
2. Wait for about ten minutes.
3. See what happens!

Isn't that incredible? Even though you can't see yeast, it does incredible things. It makes things grow and bubble! Faith is kind of like that. Even though we can't see God, it doesn't mean he is not there! He is working when we can't see him, doing amazing things in our world and lives.

WE NEED FAITH TO FOLLOW JESUS

WEEK 6
DAY 4

Everyone who believes in him will have their sins forgiven through his name.
Acts 10:43

Read This!

"I can't believe that you actually believe in God!" said Jaxon's best friend, Tyson. "Isn't that just like believing in a fairytale? I thought that stuff was made up!"

Jaxon felt hurt and confused. Was Tyson right? How was believing in Jesus any different than believing in aliens or believing that Batman would fly into his living room? He couldn't see Jesus, so was believing in him just silly?

Jaxon didn't know what to say to Tyson, so he didn't say anything. That night, at Kid's Club, he asked his group leader that same question. "Isn't believing in Jesus like believing in a fairytale?" Jaxon asked.

His group leader sat down. "Believing in Jesus is very different than believing in a fairytale!" His leader explained. "There is good reason to believe in Jesus. The Bible, a whole book written over thousands of years, gives lots of proof that he is real. Believing in him isn't just something to think about or read about, either. It actually changes our lives! Believing in Jesus saves us from our sins. It makes us brand new!"

Jaxon smiled as his leader explained. This isn't any fairytale! This is super incredible faith.

Prayer Prompt

Do you have super incredible faith in Jesus? Say a prayer telling Jesus you believe in him.

WEEK 6
DAY 5

WE NEED FAITH TO FOLLOW JESUS

Try This!

The vowels in this sentence have gone missing! Use the color code below to find the hidden meaning.

A E I O U

_V_RY_N_ WH_
B_L__V_S _N
H_M W_LL H_V_
TH__R S_NS
F_RG_V_N THR__GH
H_S N_M_.

Answers on Page 318

WE NEED FAITH TO FOLLOW JESUS

WEEK 6
DAY 6

Try This!

Believing in Jesus means having super incredible faith! If you had to make an advertisement for TV, a magazine, or the internet to encourage people to have super incredible faith, what would it look like? What would it say? Use this page to design your ad!

WEEK 7
DAY 1

TO FOLLOW JESUS, WE NEED TO FIGHT SIN

Now repent of your sins and turn to God, so that your sins may be wiped away.

Acts 3:19

Read This!

Christopher and Caylee played together at the park after school. As they were sitting on one of the benches, another kid walked by. They didn't know the kid, but right away, he started to throw garbage on the ground. He used bad language, pushed a little boy, and yelled at his mom.

"Hey, Christopher, do you think he's sinning?" asked Caylee. She didn't really know what sinning meant, but it was a word she heard at church the week before. It seemed like it meant when you did something really bad or were really mean, just like this guy was being.

"He probably is," said Christopher. "But, we all do!" Caylee was shocked! She couldn't imagine that she could sin. She didn't throw garbage on the ground. She didn't push other kids or use bad language. What did he mean?

Before she got a chance to ask, Christopher continued talking. "Everyone sins. Sin is anytime we do anything that makes God sad. It can be really mean, like what that boy is doing, but it can be small, too. It can be when we don't do the right thing, when we ignore God's plan for us, or when we don't keep him first. We all do it."

That seemed sad to Caylee. "Well, what do we do about, Christopher? It seems pretty hopeless!"

He smiled. "Mom told me the solution this week. It comes from putting Jesus in charge of your life. Telling him you're sorry and asking him for his help means we can stand up against sin! Let's do it together."

Fear Buster

Sometimes, we can be scared that we are going to do the wrong thing. With Jesus' help, we can do the right thing and stand strong against sin, even when it's tough!

TO FOLLOW JESUS, WE NEED TO FIGHT SIN

WEEK 7
DAY 2

Try This!

Here's a picture of a superhero! Color this superhero. Then, ask your parents to help find an old photo of you and cut your face out. Stick your face on this superhero, and write these words next to them: "I can stand against sin!"

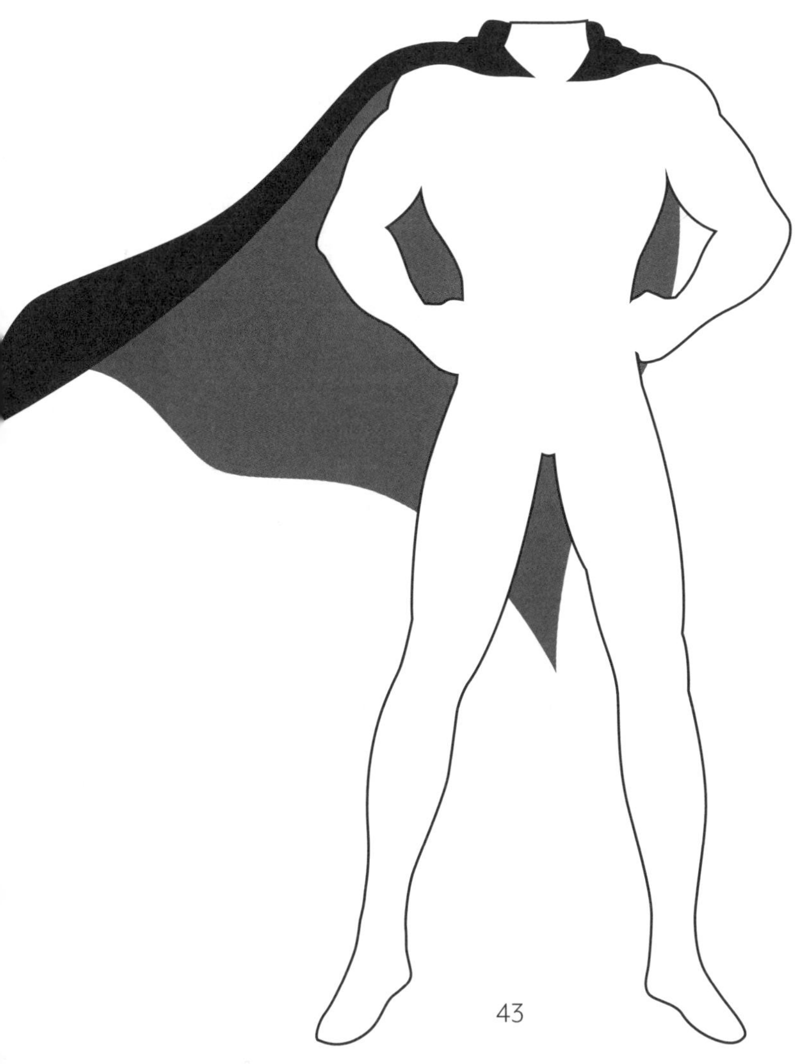

WEEK 7
DAY 3

TO FOLLOW JESUS, WE NEED TO FIGHT SIN

Try This!

The words to the verse Acts 3:19 are inside this word search. Circle them as you find them! Write the full verse on the lines below.

H	A	H	K	F	I	L	A	A	Z	U	U	F	J	U	P	B	Z
H	Z	V	S	D	G	W	U	X	T	V	Y	E	F	M	A	Y	N
G	C	I	X	Q	N	L	I	V	D	Z	F	A	A	X	Y	L	Z
M	N	R	D	P	T	X	T	P	N	V	Y	Q	I	A	A	U	U
B	W	J	J	J	F	L	H	R	E	C	J	S	S	W	K	I	T
W	Q	S	I	N	S	A	X	R	E	D	I	P	E	K	N	Q	F
F	G	S	U	A	K	E	S	W	N	P	X	S	O	B	D	J	M
W	V	B	B	W	L	A	I	B	I	E	E	M	B	X	Q	I	I
N	Q	J	S	A	U	T	D	Q	H	T	F	N	G	R	G	E	W
V	O	K	J	Y	T	U	R	N	F	L	J	G	T	O	H	M	A
C	W	W	Y	K	W	L	A	H	O	N	U	F	Z	W	D	E	V
Q	I	P	Y	O	U	R	Q	X	K	L	V	W	F	B	P	U	I

Away	Now	Turn
God	Repent	Wiped
May	Sins	Your

____

____

____

Answers on Page 318

TO FOLLOW JESUS, WE NEED TO FIGHT SIN

WEEK 7
DAY 4

If we confess our sins to him, he is faithful and just to forgive us our sins and to cleanse us from all wickedness.

1 John 1:9

Read This!

Alex stared at the chocolate-milk-stained card in his hands. His older brother, Riley had let him borrow his favorite hockey card for show-and-tell.

Alex promised to take care of the card and not let anyone touch it. But when he got to school, all his friends wanted to see it. He was sure they would be careful, too, so he started passing it around his class. Then, disaster struck! One of his buddies spilled chocolate milk all over the card. It was ruined. What was he going to do?

He had two options, he thought. He could hide it and hope Riley would forget, or he could just tell the truth and hope Riley wasn't too mad. He thought about what he would do all the way home from school.

When he arrived home, and saw Riley's smile, he knew he had to tell the truth, even if it was hard.

Alex barely had the words out when he started to cry. "I'm so sorry, Riley!"

To Alex's surprise, Riley didn't get angry. Instead, Riley hugged Alex and said, "I forgive you, Alex. Everyone makes mistakes."

Whoa! Alex wasn't expecting that. The way Riley treated Alex was the same way that Jesus treated him. Riley had made lots of mistakes, and he told Jesus many times about them. Instead of being mad and holding it against him, Jesus forgave him! He took care of all those sins for Riley and showed him love. He will do the same for all of us. All we have to do is be willing to confess when we make a mistake and do wrong.

Prayer Prompt

Do you have any sins you need to admit to Jesus? Do it now! You can be sure he will forgive you.

WEEK 7
DAY 5

TO FOLLOW JESUS, WE NEED TO FIGHT SIN

Try This!

Admitting the things we've done wrong isn't always easy, but Jesus tells us it's an important step in putting him in charge of our lives. Write a letter to Jesus telling him some of the things you've done wrong. Ask him for forgiveness, believing that he has already forgiven you. This is called confessing. After you've written it, pray and ask Jesus to forgive you. Then, write the word "FORGIVEN" across the page! It's true: When you ask, Jesus forgives!

TO FOLLOW JESUS, WE NEED TO FIGHT SIN

WEEK 7
DAY 6

Try This!

Here are some road signs! Match them up with the phrases on the other side. What can they remind us about sin?

PUT GOD IN CHARGE

DON'T LET SIN IN

STOP SINNING

TURN AWAY FROM SIN

FOLLOW JESUS ONLY

WEEK 8
DAY 1

COMMIT TO SERVING JESUS

> *We will serve the Lord our God. We will obey him alone.*
>
> Joshua 24:24

Read This!

Jordan plopped down on the couch after a long day at school. Sometimes, following Jesus was tough! Today at recess, his friends had started making fun of someone's new haircut, and they wanted him to join in. When he refused, they started making fun of him.

On the way home on the bus, some kids started yelling curse words. Everyone seemed to think they were so cool. It was tempting to join in. Jordan didn't understand why it seemed like God's way was so hard!

Even though following Jesus seemed hard, Jordan knew that it was worth it. The love that Jesus showed him was amazing! He could go to Jesus any time with any problem. Plus, his mom always reminded him that Jesus had a big plan for his life, if he just kept following his ways.

Maybe some days you feel like Jordan. Following Jesus and his ways isn't easy. Remember that even when it's hard—following God's way is worth it! He knows best, and following him is the best life there is. His plans are amazing. We just need to follow them!

Fear Buster

Following God's ways can be tough. We may feel left out, or even get made fun of. When you feel scared of following God's ways, remember that his way is the best way! We can be sure that when we obey Jesus, he will be with us. No need to be afraid!

COMMIT TO SERVING JESUS

WEEK 8
DAY 2

Try This!

God's ways are so different than the ways that many people in our world live. On this page, circle the ways that would honor God. Scratch out the ones that don't! Write in some other ideas that will help you honor God. Decide today you will follow God's ways!

BEING KIND TO A STRANGER

MAKING FUN OF SOMEONE

YELLING AT A PARENT

SHARING WITH A SIBLING

CHEATING ON A TEST

READING YOUR BIBLE

WEEK 8
DAY 3

COMMIT TO SERVING JESUS

Try This!

Fill in the blanks below to write your own story about following God's ways. Try asking someone else to fill in the blanks to get a different story each time! (Hint: A verb is an action word. An adjective is a describing word.)

I (verb______________) following God's ways! Sometimes, following God's ways is (adjective ________________). People can (verb ______________). Even though sometimes following God can make me feel (feeling word ________________), it is always worth it!

To follow God's ways, I can (verb ________________). The Bible can teach me about following God's ways. When I follow God's ways, I can ask him to (verb ___________) me.

I want to follow God's ways until I am (number____________). Someone who can help me follow God's ways is (person ________________).

COMMIT TO SERVING JESUS

WEEK 8
DAY 4

If any of you wants to be my follower, you must give up your own way, take up your cross daily, and follow me.

Luke 9:23

Read This!

One day, Jesus was walking with his disciples and they were talking about what it truly means to follow him.

"If you really want to follow me," Jesus said, "You must give up your own way of doing things." The disciples furrowed their brows and looked at each other.

"We've already left our families and homes to follow you," one disciple pointed out.

Jesus shook his head, "To follow me, you must take up your cross."

What did that mean? They thought following him would be easy. It would always be fun and amazing, with miracles and healing like it had been already.

Jesus knew that sometimes following him would be hard. People wouldn't like it, and they would laugh or make fun of his followers. Sometimes, it would be very unpopular. And sometimes, his followers would want to disobey his ways. That is why he was saying these words.

Jesus' disciples had to give up their own ways, which meant putting God's ways first. Even if they wanted to go their way, they would choose to go God's way. Even when following Jesus was hard, they would keep following him!

That was a tough challenge, but it was a part of having super incredible faith. It still is! Jesus asks us to live for him, no matter what. Sometimes it means denying ourselves, but Jesus will always help us do that. You can have that super faith. Will you follow him no matter what?

Prayer Prompt

Ask Jesus to give you the courage to have faith that follows him, no matter what!

WEEK 8
DAY 5

COMMIT TO SERVING JESUS

Try This!

How can you deny yourself? Write some ideas on this cross! Use some of the ideas below.

Pray instead of play video games

Spend time reading my Bible instead of watching TV

Be kind to someone nobody else is kind to

Keep going to Kid's Church or Sunday school when none of my friends are

Walk away from my friends when they are being bullies

Get up early for church even when I want to sleep in

COMMIT TO SERVING JESUS

WEEK 8
DAY 6

Try This!

Super heroes have to send secret messages all the time, and you can too! Morse Code is a series of dots and dashes that people use to send secret messages. Use the Morse code chart on the side to figure out the message of the gospel here:

--• •• •••- • ••- •--• -•-- --- ••- •-•

____ ____ ____ ____   ____ ____   ____ ____ ____ ____

--- •-- -•   •-- •- -•-- •••

____ ____ ____   ____ ____ ____ ____

•- -• -••

____ ____ ____

••-• --- •-•• •-•• --- •--

____ ____ ____ ____ ____ ____

-- •

____ ____

A	•-	N	-•
B	-•••	O	---
C	-•-•	P	•--•
D	-••	Q	--•-
E	•	R	•-•
F	••-•	S	•••
G	--•	T	-
H	••••	U	••-
I	••	V	•••-
J	•---	W	•--
K	-•-	X	-••-
L	•-••	Y	-•--
M	--	Z	--••

Answers on Page 318

WEEK 9 DAY 1

MY LIFE CHANGES WHEN I FOLLOW JESUS

> *Anyone who belongs to Christ has become a new person. The old life is gone; a new life has begun!*
>
> 2 Corinthians 5:17

Read This!

Chrissy's favorite time of year was getting ready to go back to school. Even though she didn't always like school (and she really didn't like getting up early!), she loved picking out new school supplies. She loved the point on newly sharpened pencils, the boldness of new markers, and the fresh new pages in her notebooks.

Owning something new was special!

We all love to own something new, whether it is school supplies, a new toy, or new clothes. Did you know that when we follow Jesus, we don't just own something new, but we become brand new?

The Bible tells us that when we decide to follow Jesus, he changes our lives, making us brand new! All of our sin is gone, and we have a fresh start. He gives us his Holy Spirit, who lives inside of us, helping us follow him. We are brand new creations when we follow Jesus. Now that is super incredible!

Fear Buster

Sometimes, we can feel like we will never be good enough to follow Jesus! Thankfully, it's not up to us! Because of the Holy Spirit, Jesus makes us brand new. We don't have to be afraid of not being good enough. He does the work for us!

MY LIFE CHANGES WHEN I FOLLOW JESUS

WEEK 9
DAY 2

Try This!

Have you ever heard of metamorphosis? It's what happens to caterpillars when they become butterflies! Look at these pictures of metamorphosis and color them. The caterpillar becomes brand new, just like we do when we follow Jesus! How are you made new by following him? Write some ideas below.

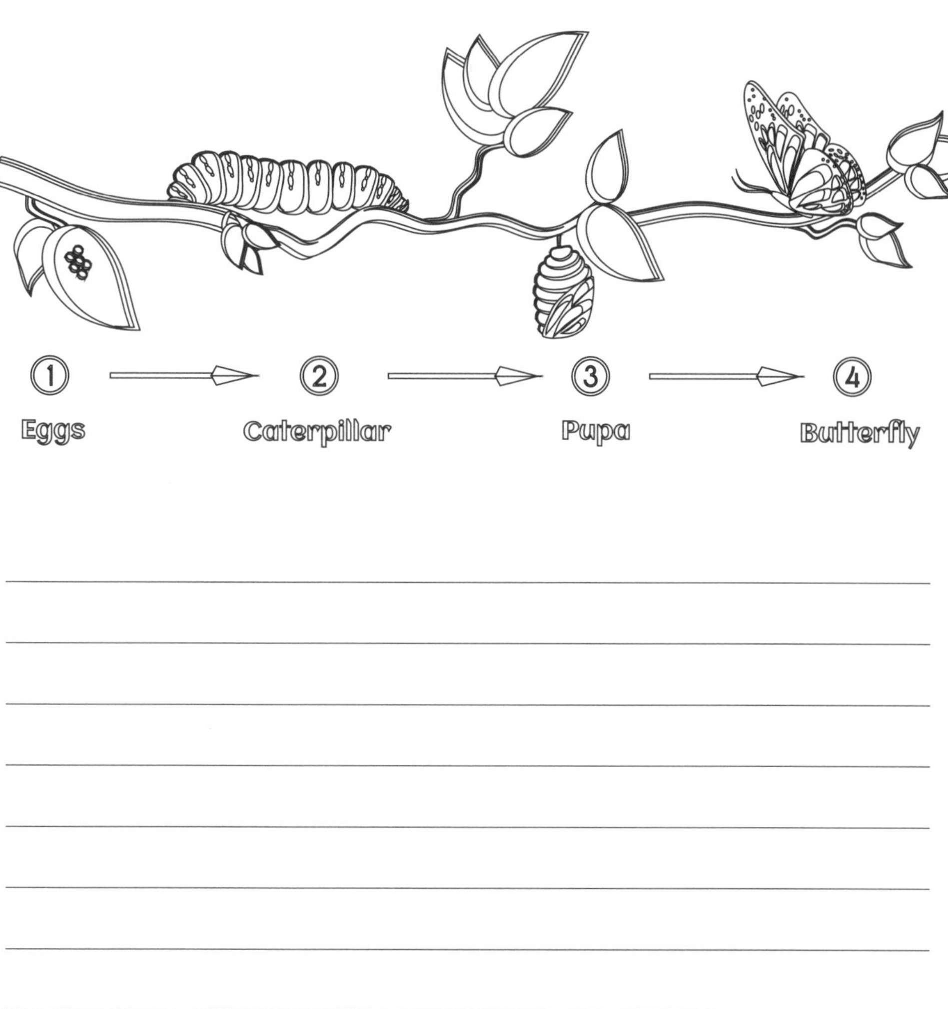

WEEK 9
DAY 3

MY LIFE CHANGES WHEN I FOLLOW JESUS

Try This!

Find some modeling clay or building blocks. Use what you have to create something brand-new. Let your imagination soar! After you've made it, write about how God has made you new!

MY LIFE CHANGES WHEN I FOLLOW JESUS

WEEK 9
DAY 4

Throw off your old sinful nature and your former way of life, which is corrupted by lust and deception. Instead, let the Spirit renew your thoughts and attitudes.

Ephesians 4:22-23

Read This!

"Grandpa, I'll never be able to live like other Christians. It's just too hard!" Jess said after Sunday school one morning.

Jess had watched the Christians in her life—her Sunday school teacher, her Grandpa, the teenage helper in her class. Their lives seemed so perfect compared to hers.

Jess's Grandpa gave her a pat on the back.

"You're right, sweetie," Grandpa responded. "It's true that you'll never be able to live like Christ on your own. None of us can."

Grandpa opened his Bible and turned the pages to a verse in Ephesians. "This verse says to let the Holy Spirit renew you. Do you know what that means?"

Jess shook her head no.

"When you follow Jesus," he explained, "the Holy Spirit starts to work in your heart. He starts to make you more like Jesus. You don't have to do it on your own!"

What a relief for Jess, and what a relief for you and me! We don't have to be perfect all the time when we follow Jesus. It's the Holy Spirit, God at work in us, that makes us new. He helps us live this brand new life with super power!

Prayer Prompt

Ask the Holy Spirit to help you live your life for Jesus!

WEEK 9
DAY 5

MY LIFE CHANGES WHEN I FOLLOW JESUS

Try This!

Here's a garbage can! The verse we read in Ephesians yesterday tells us to throw away our old ways and to let the Holy Spirit make us new! Choose some words from the word bank of things you need to 'throw away' in your life, and write them somewhere on the trash can. When you're done, pray and ask Jesus to help you!

Mean Words
Jealousy
Pride
Disobeying
Bullying
Lying
Stealing
Fighting
Gossip
Anger

BONUS ACTIVITY
Go through your closet and toy box. Throw out broken items and give away things you don't use anymore. Your room will look nice and new, too!

Try This!

Use your brain! Inside this brain, write some things you should start thinking about when you follow Jesus. Then, color the picture!

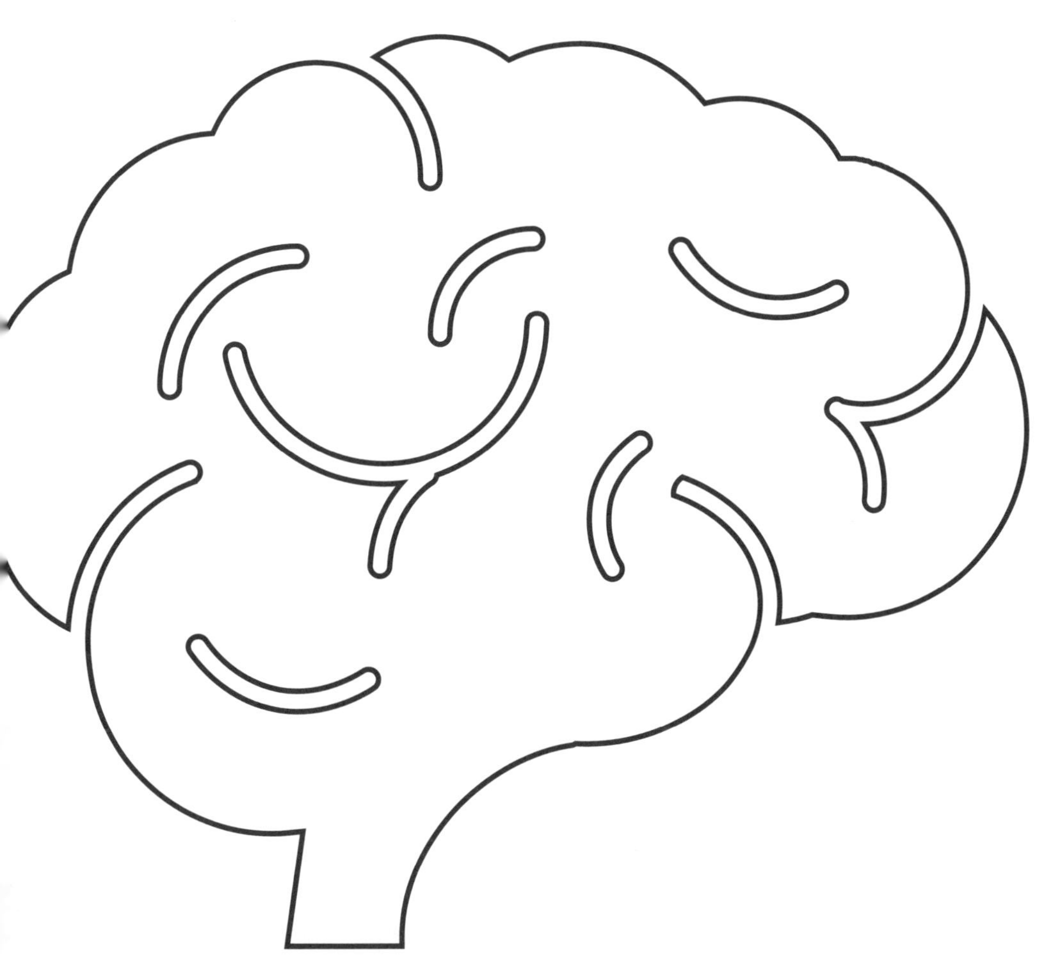

WEEK 10
DAY 1

THE BIBLE IS GOD'S GUIDE FOR LIFE

Your word is a lamp to guide my feet and a light for my path.

Psalm 119:105

Read This!

"Story time!" Trent's mom declared as she sat down on his bed.

Trent bounced up and down next to her. "Read 'Jack and the Beanstalk' again! It's my favorite."

But Mom did not pick up the book of fairytales. Instead, she picked up a thick black book.

"I know you like that story because of the giants, but there is a story in the Bible that also has a giant."

"The story of David and Goliath?" Trent asked. He remembered learning about it in Sunday School. "I like that one, too!"

"It's even better than 'Jack and the Beanstalk' because it actually happened. The Bible is filled with true stories and instructions for life. All the small books inside are part of one big book. And the point of it all is to tell God's story."

Have you ever thought about the Bible as telling God's super incredible true story? Well, that is exactly what it's for! God gave us the Bible as an amazing gift. When we read it, we can know God's plan and his great story.

Fear Buster

The Bible is God's guide for life! When we don't know what to do, we can find direction in the Bible, God's amazing story.

THE BIBLE IS GOD'S GUIDE FOR LIFE

WEEK 10
DAY 2

Try This!

The Bible is made up of sixty-six incredible books! Choose your favorite one, or pick one from a list, and answer the following questions about that book. Look up the answers in a study Bible, or research them online. You might learn something you didn't know about the Bible!

TITLE: ______________________________

OLD TESTAMENT OR NEW TESTAMENT: ______________________________

AUTHOR (IF KNOWN): ______________________________

GENRE: ______________________________

TOTAL NUMBER OF CHAPTERS: ______________________________

WHO IS IT ABOUT?

____

____

____

WHAT IS IT ABOUT?

____

____

____

FAVORITE VERSE:

____

____

WEEK 10
DAY 3

THE BIBLE IS GOD'S GUIDE FOR LIFE

Try This!

Use your imagination and what you know about the Bible to write a short story about why you think God gave us the Bible. After you've read your story, check out 2 Timothy 3:16–17. This tells us the true story of why God gave us the Bible.

THE BIBLE IS GOD'S GUIDE FOR LIFE

WEEK 10
DAY 4

For the word of God is alive and powerful. It is sharper than the sharpest two-edged sword.

Hebrews 4:12

Read This!

Stop for a minute and think about the best book you have ever read. Maybe it was a story that made you laugh out loud, a real-life tale of someone you admire, or a chapter book you just love!

Whatever the book, I'm sure it's special to you for a lot of reasons.

No matter how much you love that book, it cannot come close to being as special as the Bible is. In fact, the Bible is different than any other book that has ever been written. Why?

Because it is God's book. God used people throughout history to write down the words he wanted to share with me and you. The words inside of the Bible are meant to teach us, help us, and tell us about God. They aren't just words in another boring book. They are alive!

That means those words speak to all of us because of God's amazing power. They can help us in different situations, and they have meaning for us even though they were written thousands of years ago. What an amazing book to help us in our journey of super incredible faith!

Prayer Prompt

Thank God for the gift of an amazing, living book—the Bible.

THE BIBLE IS GOD'S GUIDE FOR LIFE

Try This!

Our Bible verse yesterday describes the Word of God as “sharper than any two-edged sword.” Scissors are like two swords tied together. With your scissors, cut out strips of paper and write Bible verses or words of encouragement for people you know. Or even people you don’t know! Hand them out to your friends or slide them in your neighbor’s mailboxes as a secret encouragement. Let your words be sharp!

THE BIBLE IS GOD'S GUIDE FOR LIFE

WEEK 10
DAY 6

Try This!

Let's memorize this Bible verse! Draw symbols or pictures on this page to help you remember the verse!

For the word of God is alive and powerful. It is sharper than the sharpest two-edged sword.

Hebrews 4:12

WEEK 11
DAY 1

I NEED TO READ THE BIBLE

> *I have hidden your word in my heart, that I might not sin against you.*
> Psalm 119:11

Read This!

Jacob sighed as he looked down at his math test. Why couldn't he remember any of the answers? He had studied so hard! He glanced over at Kristen's desk. She was flying through the questions.

Kristen was so smart. If he leaned over a little bit, he could see her paper and copy her answers. It would be so easy! He would get a good grade, and his mom and dad would be so proud.

Just as Jacob was about to start copying, a thought popped in his mind. "Do not steal." Where did that come from? His palms started getting a little sweaty, and he thought back to when he had memorized the Ten Commandments a few weeks ago. They did say not to steal. But copying answers wasn't really stealing—was it? It was no big deal!

Then, another verse came to his mind, one he had read the night before from Luke 16:11. It was just as important to be honest about little things as it was to be honest about big things. He started to get the message. God was speaking to him through his word. He wouldn't cheat on the test. He would try his best and see what happened! It was better to obey God's word!

Fear Buster

When you are in situations where you don't know what to do, God's word can help and guide you! Reading it and knowing it helps us fight sin, temptation, and hard times!

I NEED TO READ THE BIBLE

WEEK 11
DAY 2

Try This!

Color this heart and the words of Psalm 119:11. Read it over several times, and work hard to remember it! This is a super incredible truth! God's word in our heart helps us stand strong!

I have hidden your word in my heart, that I might not sin against you.

Psalm 119:11

I NEED TO READ THE BIBLE

Try This!

Complete this crossword! The answers are all characteristics of the Bible.

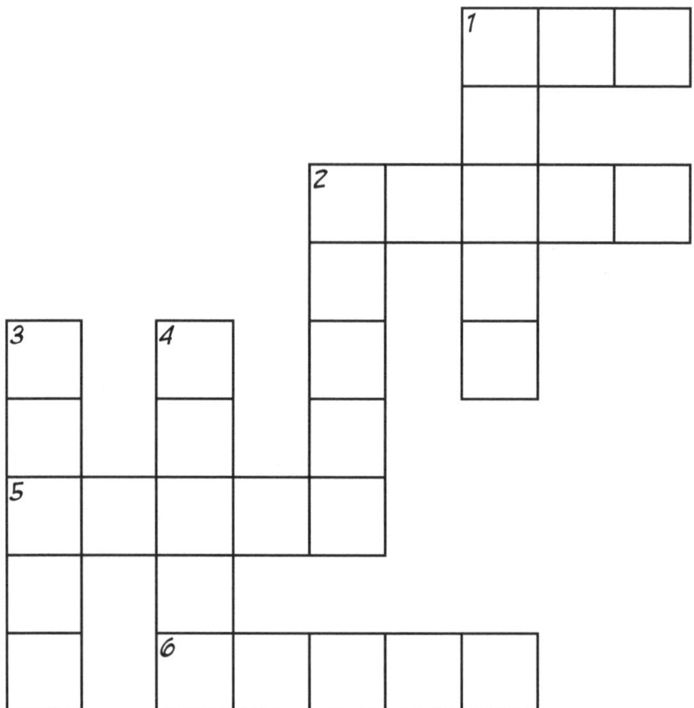

Across

1. Knowing God's Word helps us not to ________.
2. The Bible has sixty-six of these.
5. The Bible isn't a dead book, it is __________.
6. Where to hide God's Word.

Down

1. The Bible tells us God's __________.
2. God's special book for us.
3. Hebrews describes the Bible as ________er than a sword.
4. Knowing God's Word helps us have super, incredible ________.

Answers on Page 318

I NEED TO READ THE BIBLE

WEEK 11

DAY 4

All Scripture is inspired by God and is useful to teach us what is true and to make us realize what is wrong in our lives. It corrects us when we are wrong and teaches us to do what is right.

2 Timothy 3:16

Read This!

Melissa had some serious questions about following Jesus. What were the "fruit of the Spirit" that her Kids' Church teacher kept talking about? How was she supposed to pray? What happened if she did something wrong? Would her journey with following Jesus end?

These questions were on her mind a lot, especially when she was in bed at night. She wished she could find some answers somewhere. If only there was a video she could watch or a book she could check out of the library.

While there is no video that can teach you how to follow Jesus, we have been given a guide! Melissa discovered that guide, and so can you. That guide is the Bible, and all we have to do is read it. Reading the Bible helps us know how to follow Jesus.

The Bible contains all kinds of things: stories about people who followed Jesus in the past, instructions to teach us how to live, and letters that were written to tell us about who Jesus is and what he did for us! It is our guidebook for following Jesus and for life.

All Melissa had to do (and all you have to do!) is open it up and read it. As you do, God will grow your super incredible faith! Pick up your Bible and read it today.

Prayer Prompt

Thank God for the incredible gift of the Bible! Ask him to help you understand as you read it.

I NEED TO READ THE BIBLE

Try This!

Read this passage of the Bible from Luke 6:46-49. As you read, doodle or draw along the side.

So why do you keep calling me 'Lord, Lord!' when you don't do what I say? I will show you what it's like when someone comes to me, listens to my teaching, and then follows it. It is like a person building a house who digs deep and lays the foundation on solid rock. When the floodwaters rise and break against that house, it stands firm because it is well built. But anyone who hears and doesn't obey is like a person who builds a house right on the ground, without a foundation. When the floods sweep down against that house, it will collapse into a heap of ruins.

I NEED TO READ THE BIBLE

WEEK 11
DAY 6

Try This!

Life can be as confusing as a maze. But God's Word will guide you to the right choice. As you make your way through this maze, think of all the promises he made to those of us who follow Jesus.

Answers on Page 318

PRAYER CONNECTS ME TO GOD

WEEK 12
DAY 1

Read This!

> *Ask me and I will tell you remarkable secrets you do not know about things to come.*
>
> Jeremiah 33:3

It was the summer after sixth grade, and Emily had just gotten her first cellphone. She was so excited! It was so cool to be able to talk to her friends with text messages and video chats. Even though she only had a few numbers in her phone, talking to those friends was a huge treat!

She loved to be able to talk to them about her day, what she was doing tomorrow, and the new books she was reading.

One night after dinner, Emily's mom sat down with her and said, "Emily, do you know you can talk to God just like you talk to your friends on your new phone?"

Emily was confused. Sure, she prayed each night before bed, but it was nothing like talking to her friends! She could talk to her friends about anything. She just talked to God about church stuff.

Emily's mom continued, "Praying isn't meant to be just for sometimes or about certain things. God tells us in the Bible to talk to him at all times about anything! And he tells us when we talk to him, he'll answer us!"

Wow! Emily could hardly believe it. Had she been missing a chance to talk to God all this time? That night as she sat on her bed, she started to pray. This time, she prayed differently than she ever had. She told God about her day. She told him that she was scared to start junior high next month. She asked him why the words in the Bible were so long. She told him everything!

Fear Buster

No matter what situation you are in, you can talk to God! He wants to talk to you at anytime, anywhere, and about anything.

PRAYER CONNECTS ME TO GOD

WEEK 12
DAY 2

Try This!

Use the letters in the word P R A Y to write some needs you want to pray for. After you're done, take a few minutes and talk to God about them!

P ______________________________

R ______________________________

A ______________________________

Y ______________________________

WEEK 12 DAY 3

PRAYER CONNECTS ME TO GOD

Try This!

Create a comic that shows a kid just like you talking to God. Draw speech bubbles, and write a prayer need or two! God hears your prayers.

PRAYER CONNECTS ME TO GOD

WEEK 12
DAY 4

Are any of you suffering hardships? You should pray. Are any of you happy? You should sing praises. Are any of you sick? You should call for the elders of the church to come and pray over you.
James 5:13-14

Read This!

Isaiah was sitting on the hospital bed waiting for the doctor to come in. He had fallen off his bike on the way home from school, and it looked like he was going to need a cast. He was in a lot of pain!

Elizabeth had just won the gold medal in her school's swimming competition! She was so excited and proud because she had never won anything before.

Taylor was sitting in detention. She had been talking in class again. Her teacher had given her so many warnings, and now she had to stay after school. She was so embarrassed, she felt like crying.

All of these kids were in very different situations! One was hurting, one was happy, and one was embarrassed. Even though what they did was very different, they all had one thing in common. They all decided to pray.

While Isaiah sat on his hospital bed, he asked God to give him strength and to heal his leg.

Elizabeth said a prayer of thanks to God for helping her swim so well!

Taylor asked God to forgive her for not listening, and to give her power to obey.

Just like these kids, you can pray anywhere, at any time. No matter what the situation, God hears us when we pray!

Prayer Prompt

No matter what is happening in your life today, take a few minutes to pray! You can thank God, ask him for help, or say just about anything! He hears us when we talk to him.

WEEK 12
DAY 5

PRAYER CONNECTS ME TO GOD

Try This!

Fill out this story to remind you when you can pray!

Sometimes, it is (adjective __________) to pray. Other times, it is (adjective __________).

I can pray anytime! I can pray on (day ______________). I can pray (time ______________). I can pray when it is (weather word ________________). I can even pray on (holiday ______________).

I can also pray anywhere. I can pray in the (mode of transportation ______________). I can pray when I am playing (game ________________). Even when I am doing (subject ______________), I can pray.

God wants me to pray when I am (feeling ______________). He wants me to pray when I am doing (activity ______________). He is always listening! I can tell him about (noun ____________) or (person ______________). He always hears when I pray!

PRAYER CONNECTS ME TO GOD

WEEK 12
DAY 6

Try This!

Fill in what you are doing at each time in the day on this clock. (Example: 8:00, getting up for school; 6:00, eating dinner). After you fill it in, remember that you can pray at any of those times! Write down some things you can pray for at these times.

WEEK 13
DAY 1

I CAN PRAY SUPER INCREDIBLE PRAYERS

> Our Father in Heaven, may your name be kept holy. May your Kingdom come soon. May your will be done on Earth, as it is in Heaven.
>
> Matthew 6:9-10

Read This!

Jesus' followers were very confused. They had been following Jesus for a while now, and they wanted to know how to pray like he did! He didn't pray like the other people they had heard.

Jesus didn't use big words or fancy phrases. It seemed like he talked to God just like he was talking to an old friend. They wanted to know how he did it so they could do it too! When they asked Jesus to teach them to pray, he taught them the Lord's Prayer.

Maybe you have heard the Lord's Prayer at church or Sunday school. Each part of it teaches us something different about God!

Jesus started his prayer by talking to God: "Our Father in Heaven!" This reminded Jesus' followers (and us, too!) that God is in charge. He lives in Heaven and his name is holy. That means it is set apart and above everything else.

Next, Jesus asked that God would send his Kingdom and that his will would be done on Earth. Jesus knew that God's plans were bigger than ours, and he wanted his big ways to be seen on Earth.

We serve an amazing God! When we pray, we remember how incredibly big and holy he is.

Fear Buster

No need to fear when our amazing God is here! Remembering that God is in Heaven tells us he is in control. We have nothing to be scared of.

I CAN PRAY SUPER INCREDIBLE PRAYERS

WEEK 13
DAY 2

Try This!

Make a paper chain to help you remember the Lord's prayer! Write one of these phrases on each loop of paper. Draw a picture to go along with it. Hang it up in your room to help you remember the prayer each night!

OUR FATHER IN HEAVEN, MAY YOUR NAME BE KEPT HOLY.

MAY YOUR KINGDOM COME SOON.

MAY YOUR WILL BE DONE ON EARTH, AS IT IN HEAVEN.

GIVE US TODAY THE FOOD WE NEED,

AND FORGIVE US OUR SINS AS WE HAVE FORGIVEN THOSE WHO SIN AGAINST US.

AND DON'T LET US YIELD TO TEMPTATION, BUT RESCUE US FROM THE EVIL ONE.

Matthew 6:9-13

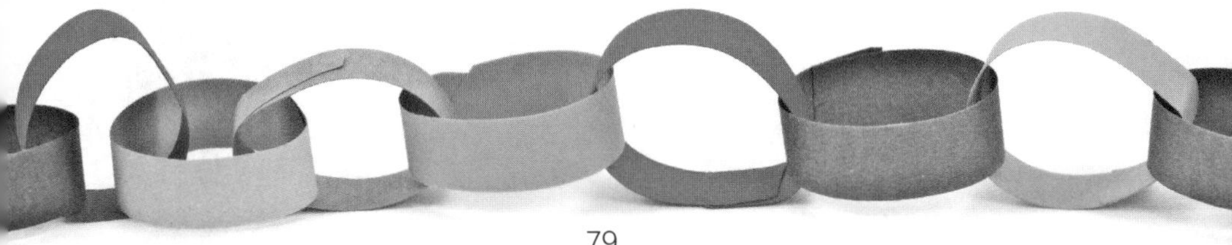

WEEK 13
DAY 3

I CAN PRAY SUPER INCREDIBLE PRAYERS

Try This!

Grab a measuring tape or a ruler! Find these items around your house and measure them. Record the numbers here.

COUCH: ______________________________

FRIDGE: ______________________________

MIRROR: ______________________________

WINDOW: ______________________________

DOOR: ______________________________

RUG: ______________________________

TABLE: ______________________________

No matter how big these items are, they don't compare to how BIG and amazing our God is!

I CAN PRAY SUPER INCREDIBLE PRAYERS

WEEK 13
DAY 4

Give us today the food we need, and forgive us our sins, as we have forgiven those who sin against us. And don't let us yield to temptation, but rescue us from the evil one.
Matthew 6:11-13

Read This!

Chelsea was making a list of things that she needed, and it was a long one.

She needed help with her social studies project.

She needed to get along better with her younger brother.

She needed her grandma to feel better and get out of the hospital.

And she needed God's help to stop getting angry with her teacher!

When Chelsea listed out all her needs, they seemed like a lot. Would God actually care about all those things? There were so many other things he had to think about!

Chelsea remembered the prayer that Jesus taught his followers, and that they prayed for the things they needed, too! They even prayed for food! If they could pray for something as simple as food, she could pray for the simple things she needed!

She could also pray for bigger things she needed, like help to follow God and forgiveness when she did wrong. Jesus said she could!

Just like Chelsea can bring her needs to God, so can you! There is no need too big or too small to pray about. He cares about you, and the things that you are facing. When you pray, be sure to share the things you need with him.

Prayer Prompt

Today, take some time to pray for the needs in your life! Share them with God!

I CAN PRAY SUPER INCREDIBLE PRAYERS

Try This!

Today, let's make a yummy bread snack to remind us that God provides for our needs—even food.

Ingredients

- ¼ teaspoon cinnamon
- 1 teaspoon sugar
- 1 tablespoon of butter
- 1 slice of bread

Directions

1. Toast the bread.
2. While the bread is toasting, mix the cinnamon and sugar in a bowl.
3. After the bread has toasted, spread the butter on top.
4. Sprinkle the buttered toast with the cinnamon-sugar mix.

As you eat the bread, thank God for taking care of every need, even for food like bread!

Try This!

In the Lord's prayer, Jesus teaches us to ask, "don't let us yield to temptation." A temptation is when you are given an opportunity to disobey God! Survey your family and close friends.

Ask, "What is a temptation you face often?" Talk together about a solution you can use to stand strong against these temptations! Write some of the answers here.

____

____

____

____

____

____

WEEK 14
DAY 1

JESUS WANTS ME TO LIVE LIKE HIM

Read This!

The Holy Spirit produces this kind of fruit in our lives: love, joy, peace, patience, kindness, goodness, faithfulness, gentleness, and self-control. There is no law against these things!

Galatians 5:22-23

Gui lived in Brazil with his family. Every morning, Gui's papai headed to work at a local banana plantation. The work there wasn't easy. Growing the delicious bananas he enjoyed each morning for breakfast was hard work!

His papai and the many others who worked there were responsible for making sure other plants didn't grow too close to the banana trees, watering the plants, and spraying to keep insects away. Each night at dinner, Gui's papai looked exhausted from a long, hard day of work.

Yet, every night when they sat down at the dinner table, they read from the Bible. One night, as they read about the fruit of the Spirit, Gui thought about how much work growing fruit was! Seeing his dad work at the banana plantation reminded Gui that fruit didn't grow overnight. If bananas were so much work, how on Earth was he supposed to grow things like love, joy, and patience?

As they chatted about it at the supper table, Gui's family reminded him that he didn't have to grow the fruit of the Spirit on his own. In fact, he wasn't supposed to! The Holy Spirit was working in his life to make him more like Jesus, and as he grew his relationship with Jesus, those fruit would start to grow!

Gui was excited. He wanted to be more like Jesus, and was excited for the Holy Spirit to help him get there!

Fear Buster

When you feel like you can't live like Jesus, the Holy Spirit is there to help you! He makes us more like Jesus by growing the fruit of the Spirit in our lives.

JESUS WANTS ME TO LIVE LIKE HIM

WEEK 14
DAY 2

Try This!

If you were any fruit, what would you be? Take this quiz to find out!

1. *What is your favorite color?*
   A. Yellow
   B. Red
   C. Green
   D. Orange
2. *How would you describe your perfect day?*
   A. Just hanging out!
   B. Going somewhere special
   C. Being with friends
   D. Relaxing somewhere nice
3. *What is the best way to enjoy fruit?*
   A. In a smoothie
   B. On an ice-cream sundae
   C. Just like it is!
   D. As a juice
4. *If you could be any animal, what would you be?*
   A. Monkey
   B. Puppy
   C. Deer
   D. Ape
5. *Where would your perfect vacation be?*
   A. China
   B. California
   C. France
   D. Brazil

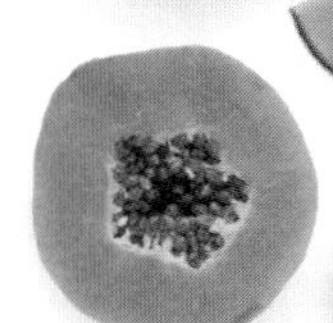

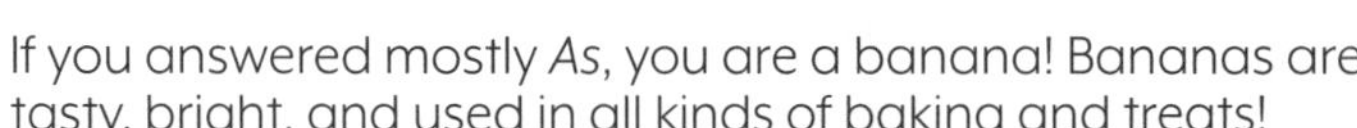

If you answered mostly *As*, you are a banana! Bananas are tasty, bright, and used in all kinds of baking and treats!

If you answered mostly *Bs*, you are a strawberry! Small and sweet, strawberries are easy to pick and even easier to eat.

If you answered mostly *Cs*, you are a grape. Grapes can be green or red, and they always grow in bunches. They grow all over the world!

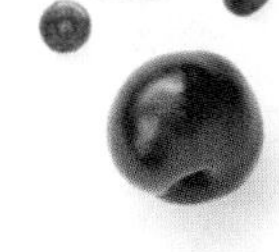

If you answered mostly *Ds*, you are an orange! Juicy and tart, oranges are a favorite for breakfast, especially that delicious freshly squeezed juice!

JESUS WANTS ME TO LIVE LIKE HIM

Try This!

Have you ever made a fruit salad? With permission from a grown-up, gather up whatever fruit you can find in your house. Some great fruits for fruit salad include berries, pineapple, peaches, and cherries (but anything goes!).

Use a knife to cut up bigger pieces of fruit, and then add some delicious toppings (whipped cream, yogurt, or jello go great with this snack).

As you add the fruit, see if you can remember all the fruit of the Spirit listed in Galatians 5. If you can't remember, go back and look at this week's devotional! Ask God to grow these fruit in your life as you enjoy your delicious snack.

JESUS WANTS ME TO LIVE LIKE HIM

WEEK 14
DAY 4

Owe nothing to anyone—except for your obligation to love one another. If you love your neighbor, you will fulfill the requirements of God's law.

Romans 13:8

Read This!

Alexander's brother, Micah, was being so annoying. Even though Alexander knew Micah was younger, and he knew that he should be nice to him, it was so hard!

Micah was always in Alexander's personal space, stealing his stuff, and worst of all, telling his friends embarrassing stories whenever they came over.

How was Alexander supposed to love someone who did that? It seemed impossible.

Have you ever felt like Alexander? Maybe there is someone in your life who is really hard to love. It may be a sibling who is always fighting with you, a kid in your class who is mean to you, or a teacher or grown-up who has really hurt you. When you think about showing them love, it seems impossible!

Thankfully, God doesn't expect us to show them love on our own! He gives us the strength of his Holy Spirit in our hearts. The Holy Spirit fills us with love that comes from God when we feel like we can't love. It's not a love like humans show. It's a love that is unconditional. That means we love like God does, even when people don't deserve it! When we show love like God, we can know he is growing the fruit of love in our lives.

Prayer Prompt

Think of someone in your life who is hard to love. Ask God to grow the fruit of love in your heart for that person!

WEEK 14
DAY 5

JESUS WANTS ME TO LIVE LIKE HIM

Try This!

Are you ready for the LOVE challenge? Use the letters of the word LOVE to come up with one way you can show love to someone over the next two days. Come back to this page to check off each thing you do to show love!

L ____________________

O ____________________

V ____________________

E ____________________

JESUS WANTS ME TO LIVE LIKE HIM

WEEK 14
DAY 6

Try This!

Sometimes, people in your family can be the hardest ones to love! Make a LOVE coupon in the space below for someone in your family. Then, trace it onto another page and give it to them. Tell them they can cash it in to you whenever you aren't being loving!

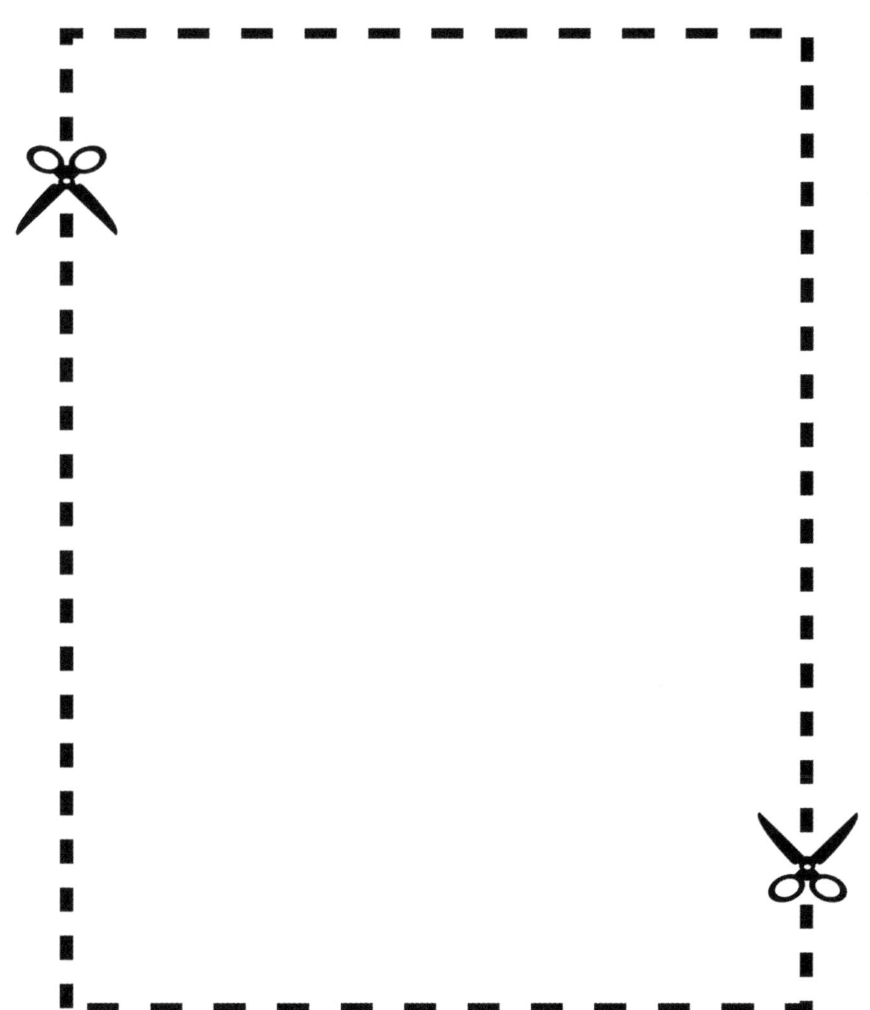

JESUS WANTS ME TO HAVE JOY AND PEACE

WEEK 15
DAY 1

Read This!

Don't be dejected and sad, for the joy of the Lord is your strength.
Nehemiah 8:10

Things were not going well for Abe.

First of all, he was struggling with math. He could never do his homework right, he felt sick to his stomach when he studied, and got so confused every time he sat at his desk.

Secondly, he had just found out his grandma was in the hospital. It seemed like nobody was telling him what was wrong, and he was sad, confused, and scared.

If all that wasn't enough, his best friend, Michael, had been acting very strangely lately. He was always busy when Abe asked him to hang out, and he had started spending time with a group of bullies at school.

Things were really hard right now. A lot of mornings when he woke up, Abe wasn't feeling happy or excited. He felt down in the dumps. How could he be happy when so many things were going wrong?

One day, as he was thinking about how tough things were, a thought crossed his mind. He thought, "Even though things are hard, God still loves me!" Where did that come from?

Somehow, he started to feel something different in his heart. It felt like . . . joy. In that moment, Abe knew that even when things were hard, he could trust in God! That gave him joy that was bigger than a bad day.

Fear Buster

When you are scared or sad, ask God to give you joy. That joy doesn't depend on what is happening around you, but on your amazing God!

JESUS WANTS ME TO HAVE JOY AND PEACE

WEEK 15
DAY 2

Try This!

Celebrations are times filled with joy! On this page below, plan your dream party. What songs would you have playing? What decorations would you display? Draw a picture to inspire your plans! As you plan your celebration, thank Jesus for the joy he gives!

MY PARTY PLANS

Music to Play

1. ______________________________

2. ______________________________

3. ______________________________

Decorations

Color: ______________________________

Theme: ______________________________

Food

1. ______________________________

2. ______________________________

3. ______________________________

Who's Coming

____

____

____

WEEK 15
DAY 3

JESUS WANTS ME TO HAVE JOY AND PEACE

Try This!

Spread some joy to the people in your life by making some JOY confetti. Grab some paper and cut it out into pieces, and then write some Bible verses on them. With a parent's permission, sprinkle the confetti on your kitchen table before your family eats dinner, on the bathroom counter, or somewhere else you think someone could use some joy! Use one of these sample verses or choose your own!

The joy of the Lord is my strength.

Nehemiah 8:10

God, the source of hope, will fill you completely with joy.

Romans 15:13

Show me the way of life, granting me the joy of your presence.

Psalm 16:11

JESUS WANTS ME TO HAVE JOY AND PEACE

WEEK 15
DAY 4

His peace will guard your hearts and minds as you live in Christ Jesus.

Philippians 4:7

Read This!

Lydia had that strange feeling in her stomach again. Her hands were sweaty, and her heart was racing. This seemed to happen a lot. Right now, it was because she was about to give a speech in front of her class.

It happened at other times too—when her parents were fighting at home, or that time when she couldn't find her mom at the mall. She wasn't quite sure how to describe it, other than she was just plain scared.

When those moments came, Lydia didn't know what to do. Sometimes she tried to imagine she was somewhere else , and sometimes it worked. Other times, she counted to ten, forward and backward. That worked sometimes, too!

What she had started doing this week was something brand new! She was praying for God to give her peace. Even though her situation didn't change, she felt God's peace in her heart anyway! It was a feeling that everything was going to be okay. All she had to do was trust God.

Have you ever felt scared or anxious like Lydia? No matter what situation you are facing, God can bring peace to your heart!

Prayer Prompt

Tell God the things that are happening in your life that make you feel scared. Ask him to give you his peace.

JESUS WANTS ME TO HAVE JOY AND PEACE

Try This!

Peace often happens in quiet moments. Go somewhere quiet (maybe your bedroom), and sit down with this page. Write a letter to God, telling him the things that are bothering you right now. Spend some time praying in the quiet, and then write down what you feel like God is saying to your heart.

JESUS WANTS ME TO HAVE JOY AND PEACE

WEEK 15
DAY 6

Try This!

There are a lot of things that can make kids feel nervous or scared! From the list here, circle the ones that make you feel scared. Write in some others, if you can think of them. Draw a line from them to the circle that says "God." Once you're done, write across the bottom of the page, "God, I give it to you!"

Schoolwork

Bullies

Family problems

Fighting

The future

Getting sick or hurt

New places

Moving

____

____

____

WEEK 16
DAY 1

JESUS WANTS ME TO BE PATIENT AND KIND

> *Since God chose you to be the holy people he loves, you must clothe yourselves with tenderhearted mercy, kindness, humility, gentleness and patience.*
>
> Colossians 3:12

Read This!

Owen was so tired of waiting to grow up!

It seemed like everything he wanted to do had to wait until he was older.

He couldn't go to the mall alone with his friends until he was in junior high. He couldn't start youth group at church until next year. His older brother and sister could both drive wherever they wanted to go, but it would be years before he learned how!

Sometimes, it seemed like everything fun and good was so far away. It was really hard to wait. Owen wasn't good at being patient.

Maybe you've felt like Owen at times. Something you're looking forward to seems like it is never going to come! Or maybe, you're waiting for God to answer a prayer or fix a problem and it seems like it will never happen.

Waiting is tough. Thankfully, we don't have to do it on our own. When we ask God, the Holy Spirit can help us to be patient, to wait and trust God, no matter what comes our way!

Fear Buster

When things seem like they are never going to happen, I can trust that God has everything under control!

JESUS WANTS ME TO BE PATIENT AND KIND

WEEK 16
DAY 2

Try This!

Sometimes it is hard to be a kid. You just want to do what the bigger kids are doing all the time. In the top of the hour-glass below, write things that you can do right now. In the bottom, write things that you want to do when you get older. Some of these "later goals" may take a long time, but with God's help, you can be patient.

JESUS WANTS ME TO BE PATIENT AND KIND

Try This!

Cooking is a great way to learn patience! Try making this pizza to practice patience. Spend time with God while it's cooking!

Ingredients

- ½ English muffin or small tortilla
- ¼ cup tomato sauce
- ⅛ cup shredded cheese
- toppings (veggies, deli meat, etc.)

Directions

1. Set your oven to 350°F.
2. Use a spoon to spread sauce on the muffin or tortilla.
3. Sprinkle your toppings and cheese over the top of the sauce.
4. Place the pizza on a baking tray and put it in the oven.
5. Set a timer for 10 minutes. This is a good time to practice your patience! Don't leave the kitchen. Instead, come up with ways to pass the time. Sing a song, talk to God, or draw a picture.
6. When the timer goes off, get a grown-up to help you remove the pizza from the oven and dig in! As you eat, remember that being patient pays off.

JESUS WANTS ME TO BE PATIENT AND KIND

WEEK 16
DAY 4

Read This!

Love is patient and kind.
1 Corinthians 13:4

Marley's friends had started to act differently over the past few weeks. When a new kid, David, had moved into their class from another country, they had started making fun of him. They made fun of the way he spoke, the clothes he wore, and even the food he ate for lunch.

Marley couldn't understand why they had started being so mean! Even though she wanted to tell them to stop, she also didn't want to get made fun of. Most of the time, she stayed quiet. But she started to feel guilty and uncomfortable.

When Marley told her mom about it, she reminded her that God wanted her to be kind! Even when it was hard to stand up to her friends or to show David kindness, if she asked God, the Holy Spirit would help her be kind.

The next day at school, Marley decided to be brave. She whispered a prayer and walked over to where David was sitting. Instead of making fun of him, she sat down beside him and started asking him questions about the place he used to live. Before she knew it, they were laughing and talking like they'd been friends forever!

Marley knew that God was helping her be kind to David. Who do you need God's help to show kindness to this week?

Prayer Prompt

Invite the Holy Spirit to help you be kind to those around you this week.

WEEK 16
DAY 5

JESUS WANTS ME TO BE PATIENT AND KIND

Try This!

It's hard being different! Write about a time you felt different. What made you feel different? How did it make you feel? How can remembering this help you love others who are different from you?

JESUS WANTS ME TO BE PATIENT AND KIND

WEEK 16
DAY 6

Try This!

Are these actions KIND or UNKIND? Put a check mark next to the kind actions. Write a kind action underneath the unkind actions.

Sitting with someone at lunch and then making fun of them when you leave.

Sharing snacks with someone who forgot theirs at recess.

Making fun of the way someone stutters when they speak in public.

Standing up for someone who is being bullied.

Acting nice to someone but not really meaning it.

Telling someone who seems alone that God loves them.

WEEK 17 DAY 1

JESUS WANTS ME TO BE FAITHFUL AND GOOD

Whenever we have the opportunity, we should do good to everyone.

Galatians 6:10

Read This!

"Can't you just be good for once!?"

"You're such a good person!"

"You did such a good job with that!"

Has anyone ever said these things to you before? We use the word "good" a lot! Being good is even one of the fruit of the Spirit.

What does that mean, though? Does it just mean being on our best behavior and not breaking the rules?

While behavior is important, goodness isn't just about listening to rules or behaving well. Goodness is about what's in our hearts! When we invite the Holy Spirit to work in our hearts, he grows God's goodness in us.

It's out of this goodness that we are able to show kindness, listen to rules, and behave the right way. We treat other people the way they should be treated and choose to do the right thing. This happens not because of us but because of God working in us! While goodness isn't always easy, it always shows God how much we love him!

WHAM!

Prayer Prompt

Ask God to fill your heart with his goodness and love.

JESUS WANTS ME TO BE FAITHFUL AND GOOD

WEEK 17
DAY 2

Try This!

Goodness is about what's in our hearts! What's in your heart? Write the good things that are in your heart inside the heart on this page. You might have some bad things in your heart, too. Write the bad things outside of the heart to show that God is working in you!

WEEK 17
DAY 3

JESUS WANTS ME TO BE FAITHFUL AND GOOD

Try This!

Unscramble the words to figure out the verse!

we good should
everyone have
do opportunity
whenever
to the we

Verse:

JESUS WANTS ME TO BE FAITHFUL AND GOOD

WEEK 17
DAY 4

If you are faithful in little things, you will be faithful in large ones.

Luke 16:10

Read This!

When Raya entered sixth grade, a lot of her friends stopped going to Kids' Church with her. They said God was for babies, and they were older now!

Allie's best friend, Mia, acted like she was a Christian on Sundays, but when they were at school, she used bad words and made fun of Allie for loving God.

Trevor's whole hockey team said they were going to gang up on him and hide away his gear if he didn't stop being such a Jesus freak.

Raya, Allie, and Trevor were all facing tough decisions. Would they continue to follow God when the going got tough? They had to decide whether or not they were going to be faithful.

As you get older, you may find it gets harder to remain faithful to God! Being faithful means staying true and sticking with it, even when it's not easy. It can be easy to be faithful when everyone else is doing it, but it's harder when you are alone or it's not popular.

The Bible tells us that God will help us remain faithful to him, and that it's always worth it. How can you be faithful this week?

Fear Buster

When being faithful is scary and unpopular, we can trust that God is with us! He promises to be faithful to us no matter what.

WEEK 17
DAY 5

JESUS WANTS ME TO BE FAITHFUL AND GOOD

Try This!

Hebrews 11 in the New Testament contains stories of many Bible characters who were faithful to God. Chose six people from Hebrews 11 and draw a picture in each square of what they did to be faithful to God.

JESUS WANTS ME TO BE FAITHFUL AND GOOD

WEEK 17
DAY 6

Try This!

Choose one of your favorite Bible characters, and create a profile of them (think about Facebook, Instagram, or even a sports profile!) showcasing how they were faithful. Draw their picture in the box and answer the questions below.

Name: ______________________________

Claim to Fame: ______________________________

Where They Lived: ______________________________

What They Did for God: ______________________________

____

Examples of Being Faithful: ______________________________

____

WEEK 18 DAY 1

JESUS WANTS ME TO HAVE GENTLENESS AND SELF-CONTROL

> *Always be humble and gentle. Be patient with each other, making allowance for each others faults because of your love.*
> Ephesians 4:2

Read This!

Have you ever held a baby? Maybe it was a little brother or sister, a cousin, or just someone you knew. When you hold a baby, you have to be very careful! You have to support their head, touch them softly, and be sure not to be rough. Babies are still so small and new. They need extra special care.

Maybe when you were holding that baby, a grown-up reminded you to be gentle. They were telling you to be sure you were soft, careful, and kind to that baby!

Did you know that God doesn't just want us to be gentle with babies, but with everyone? In fact, gentleness is another Fruit of the Spirit! Being gentle can be hard to describe, but it means showing kindness and being careful with other people's hearts and feelings.

We are being gentle when we choose to speak kindly instead of getting angry. We show gentleness when we care for other people's things. We are gentle when we watch what we say and how we say it!

Being gentle can be hard, especially when other people choose to be rough, angry, or rude. Just like all the other fruit of the Spirit, we can trust God to help us. He can grow gentleness in our lives!

Prayer Prompt

Think of a time when you needed to be gentle! Ask God to help you be gentle every time you face that situation and others like it.

Try This!

This gentleness scale ranges from one (not gentle) to five (very gentle). Read the descriptions and see where you think you fall! Circle it, and then brainstorm two ways you can try to be more gentle!

1. I get angry fast and easily! When I'm angry, I yell, say mean things, or pout.
2. If everything is going my way, I am in a good mood and kind. When things go bad, I get angry and upset, and I hurt those around me.
3. I show gentleness and kindness to those who are weaker or smaller than me, like babies, small kids ,or animals. People who are my age or older sometimes make me angry!
4. I try to be gentle whenever I can, but I don't always do a good job.
5. God is helping me show gentleness to everyone around me! I don't get angry, mean, or bossy very often!

How can I be more gentle?

____

____

JESUS WANTS ME TO HAVE GENTLENESS AND SELF-CONTROL

Try This!

Take these words and place them under the heading of either Gentle or Not Gentle. What lessons can you learn from the Gentle things?

Baby	Boss	Child
Kitten	Teacher	Bully
Grandma	Puppy	Nurse
Lion	Snake	Storm

GENTLE	NOT GENTLE

Answers on Page 318

For God has not given us a spirit of fear and timidity, but of power, love, and self-discipline.

2 Timothy 1:7

Read This!

"Hey Lexi, can I borrow your tablet?" Ryan asked his twin sister. "I want to practice that new dance they taught us at school."

Lexi glanced up from the book she was reading. "Yea, just be careful," Lexi said.

"Thanks!" Ryan bounded out of the room. A few minutes later, Lexi heard Ryan stomping and jumping in the next room.

Wow, it's sounds like he's playing the drums with his feet, Lexi thought.

SMASH! Lexi sat up in her bed. *That better not be what I think it is,* she thought. She scrambled into the next room. Ryan lay on his stomach, his arms stretched out in front of him, and the tablet's screen shattered. Lexi could feel the angry feelings bubbling up inside of her. She thought she was going to explode. If she gave in, she would yell, kick, and maybe even hit Ryan! Didn't he know how important that tablet was to her?!

Instead of losing her cool, Lexi took a couple of deep breaths. She reminded herself that God could help her have self-control. She didn't have to get angry. Instead, she could trust God and give her feelings of anger to him. That wasn't easy. It took Lexi a long time to calm down. She had to walk away, count to ten, and do a lot of praying.

After it was all over, Lexi felt good that she hadn't lost her temper at Ryan. She knew it meant that she was becoming more like Jesus. The Fruit of the Spirit was growing in her!

Fear Buster

Sometimes when we feel scared, angry, or threatened, our emotions overwhelm us! Thankfully, we don't have to face them alone. The Holy Spirit gives us self-control that can keep us calm even in tough situations.

Try This!

Sometimes it can feel like we're bubbling over with anger! How do you keep your anger under control? Try this experiment and think of ways that will help you control your anger.

Materials

- Empty water or soda bottle
- ½ cup vinegar
- ¼ cup of warm water,
- 1 ½ tablespoons baking soda

Directions

- Pour vinegar and water in the bottle. Mix well.
- Add in the baking soda.
- Watch what happens!
- As you look at the results, talk with a friend or grown-up about how you can keep from exploding when things make you upset!

Try This!

Take a look at this thermometer to determine how you're feeling today. Fill in the thermometer to the words that best describe how you feel. Where do you fall? Why do you think you're feeling that way? The examples below can help you handle your feelings!

1. Ask God to be close to you and help you control your feelings!
2. Count to ten and back!
3. Memorize this week's verse and repeat it back to yourself when you feel angry or overwhelmed.
4. Talk to someone you trust and ask them to help you figure out why you are feeling this way.
5. Breathe in and out deeply five times!
6. Come up with your own idea:

____

____

____

____

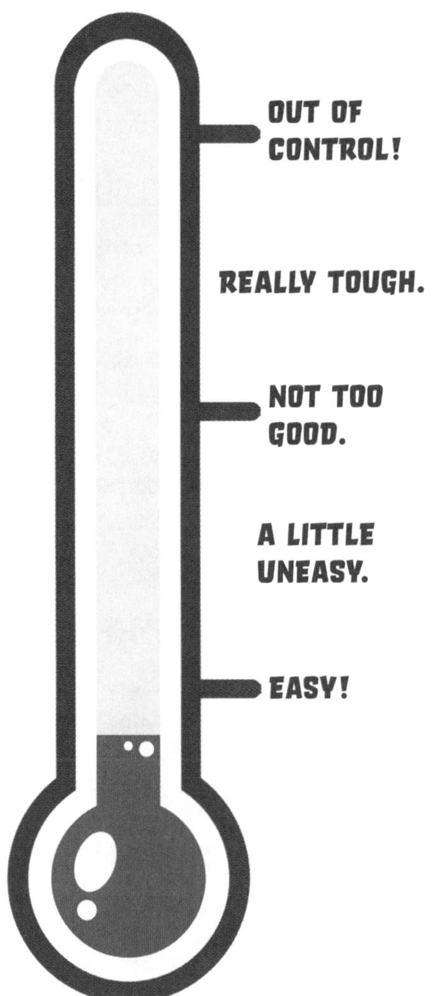

WEEK 19
DAY 1

I CAN LOVE OTHERS LIKE JESUS DID

God showed his great love for us by sending Christ to die for us while we were still sinners.

Romans 5:8

Read This!

Jack considered himself to be a pretty nice guy. He listened to his teachers, shared his extra lunch and snacks with people who forgot theirs, and he even sat with the kids that nobody liked.

There was one person though he just could not manage to be nice to, and that was Finn. He just could not stand him because he was SO mean! Finn always made fun of Jake's clothes and the way he talked, and he had even started pushing him down when they spent time outdoors at lunch.

Jack was being nice to everyone else . Why did he have to be nice to Finn?

As he sat in church on Sunday, he was reminded of why: because Jesus showed love to everyone. Jesus didn't just show love to those who deserved it. In fact, Jesus purposely loved people who didn't! Jesus loved people who were mean to him, people who disobeyed him, and even told his followers to love their enemies!

To be like Jesus, Jack knew he had to show love to Finn. He took a deep breath, and then he prayed. He would try to show God's love, but he needed Jesus to help him do it!

Prayer Prompt

Think of someone you find hard to love. Ask God to fill your heart with his love for that person!

I CAN LOVE OTHERS LIKE JESUS DID

WEEK 19
DAY 2

Try This!

Find these words of people who you can love, even when it's hard!

I	A	G	Y	C	Q	T	G	S	N	D	J	L	O	G	S	G	Q
Q	J	R	E	Z	J	K	Z	O	I	N	N	I	R	R	T	J	B
L	V	S	U	T	D	B	B	H	Y	S	T	I	Z	L	R	I	Y
Z	Z	I	W	E	S	P	R	G	H	V	T	E	C	K	A	M	N
W	E	J	C	A	T	G	D	O	V	S	L	E	N	P	N	R	H
W	N	G	A	C	T	F	N	A	T	N	A	G	R	E	G	A	T
V	E	J	H	H	F	G	R	T	R	H	I	O	A	V	E	B	E
L	M	G	C	E	Q	U	R	I	B	N	E	A	Y	Y	R	C	D
Z	Y	G	Q	R	J	P	A	R	E	N	T	R	L	L	K	D	K
U	A	T	W	B	E	W	G	G	U	N	K	I	N	E	P	Z	Q
D	B	U	L	L	Y	P	F	T	J	U	D	T	G	C	S	T	X
O	Z	A	X	O	O	C	G	K	N	O	S	I	R	A	D	L	J

Bully
Brother
Teacher
Enemy
Sister
Friend
Parent
Stranger

Answers on Page 318

I CAN LOVE OTHERS LIKE JESUS DID

Try This!

Decipher the code to figure out Jesus' message about love:

A	26
B	25
C	24
D	23
E	22
F	21
G	20
H	19
I	18
J	17
K	16
L	15
M	14
N	13
O	12
P	11
Q	10
R	9
S	8
T	7
U	6
V	5
W	4
X	3
Y	2
Z	1

15 12 5 22 2 12 6 9

22 13 22 14 18 22 8 !

11 9 26 2 21 12 9

7 19 12 8 22 4 19 12

11 22 9 8 22 24 6 7 22

2 12 6 .

Matthew 5:44

Answers on Page 318

I CAN LOVE OTHERS LIKE JESUS DID

WEEK 19
DAY 4

A friend is always loyal, and a brother is born to help in time of need.

Proverbs 17:17

Read This!

Let's be honest for a few minutes.

When you're having a good day, it's easy to love those around you!

When you are in a great mood, it's contagious. You share it with others.

When you get an *A* on your homework, it's not too hard to say you have the best teacher ever.

Other times, it's harder to show love. When your day is going horribly, you don't want to show other people love. When you're feeling grumpy or sad, you say rude things or avoid your friends.

OH!

And when you get a bad mark on your homework, it's easy to be rude to your teacher or talk about them with your friends.

The Bible teaches us that we are supposed to show love all the time. That's what Jesus did, and it's what he wants us to do! We don't just show love when we feel like it or when it's easy. We love others no matter what kind of day we are having or what mood we have.

This is a challenge, and it requires us to have super incredible faith! When you don't feel like showing love, you can call on our God who loves at all times and ask him to give you his incredible love to share with others.

Fear Buster

Sometimes, we don't show love because we are feeling scared, sad, or confused. Because of God's great love, we can show love to others no matter how we feel.

WEEK 19
DAY 5

I CAN LOVE OTHERS LIKE JESUS DID

Try This!

Imagine this is a magazine cover from the days Jesus walked on the Earth! Come up with a headline and draw a cover picture of Jesus showing love.

I CAN LOVE OTHERS LIKE JESUS DID

WEEK 19
DAY 6

Try This!

Everybody loves a good Top 10 list. Make a Top 10 list of ways you can show love. When you are having a bad or hard day, look at this list and choose one of the ways to show love, even if you don't feel like it.

1. __________

2. __________

3. __________

4. __________

5. __________

6. __________

7. __________

8. __________

9. __________

10. __________

I CAN SERVE OTHERS LIKE JESUS DID

WEEK 20
DAY 1

> *Since I, your Lord and Teacher, have washed your feet, you ought to wash each other's feet. I have given you an example to follow. Do as I have done to you.*
>
> John 13:14-15

Read This!

Jesus knew that his time to die was coming soon. He had spent three years with his closest friends, telling them about God, performing amazing miracles, and teaching them to trust in him.

As their time together came to an end, he wanted to show them how much he loved them, and he knew an amazing way he could do that.

When they met together for their last meal, he took out a bowl of water and some towels. One by one, he started washing his followers' feet.

Can you imagine how it would have felt to have Jesus wash your feet? His followers had been walking all day on dirt roads. Their feet were probably dirty—not to mention smelly! They probably felt pretty embarrassed, but also honored that Jesus, their Master, was washing their feet.

When they asked Jesus why he was doing this, he told them he wanted to show them how to serve. Just like he was serving them, they needed to serve others. Washing feet was just one example of how they could do that.

The same truth applies to us today. Jesus wants us to serve like he did! Serving other people is just one way we can show our incredible faith in him.

Fear Buster

Sometimes we can be scared to serve other people. Jesus wants us to serve just like he did, and when we do, we can know that he'll be with us!

I CAN SERVE OTHERS LIKE JESUS DID

WEEK 20
DAY 2

Try This!

It can be hard to know where to begin when it comes to serving others. To get some ideas of how you can serve, ask others how they serve! Interview three people—a parent, teacher, sibling, or friend—about the ways they serve. Record their answers below.

Name:

Ways they serve others:

Name:

Ways they serve others:

Name:

Ways they serve others:

I CAN SERVE OTHERS LIKE JESUS DID

WEEK 20
DAY 3

Try This!

Let's think of ways we can serve! Inside the left foot, brainstorm some ways that Jesus served people in the Bible. One of them we already learned about this week—washing his followers' feet. In the right foot, write ways you can serve like Jesus. Use some ideas from yesterday's activity if you feel stuck!

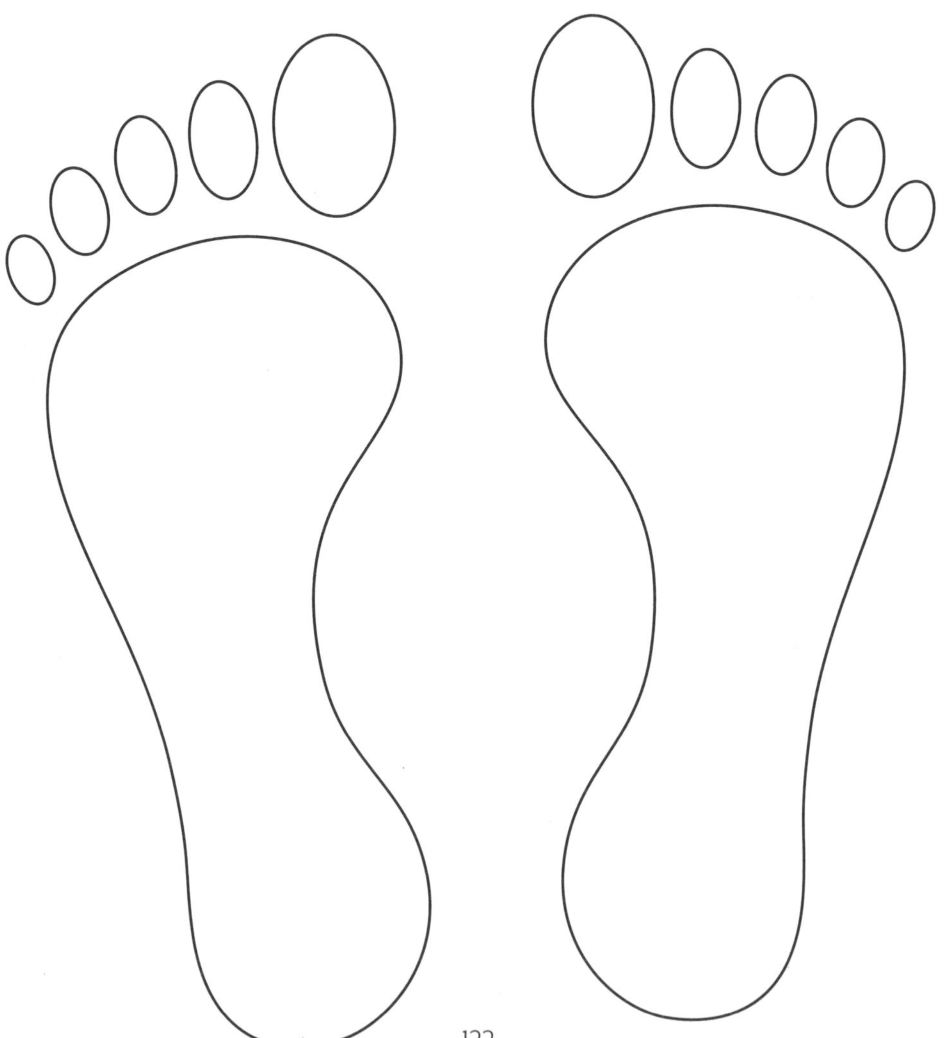

I CAN SERVE OTHERS LIKE JESUS DID

WEEK 20

DAY 4

When he appeared in human form, he humbled himself in obedience to God.

Philippians 2:7-8

Read This!

Arianna beamed at the exam in her hands. It was her second A+ in a row. Plus, last week in her gymnastics competition she had won gold. And earlier today, her teacher awarded her Student of the Week!

"I am on a roll!" she said to herself as she put her exam in her locker and headed to lunch.

Arianna was doing some awesome things! Just as she was dwelling on these thoughts, she passed by her friend, Logan. He was sitting in the cafeteria at lunchtime, looking pretty confused. She saw his math homework next to him, only half completed.

Her mind started to race. *Why didn't Logan have his homework done? If he was as smart as me, he would have it done. Why should I help Logan?*

In her heart, she knew the right thing to do. She knew that she shouldn't think she was any better than Logan just because she won some awards. If Jesus was there, he definitely would have helped Logan. And after all, she was trying to be like him!

Putting aside her pride, she pulled up a chair next to Logan and offered to help. A smile of relief came across his face—and hers, too! She was being humble and serving like Jesus!

Prayer Prompt

Ask God to help you keep from having pride in your heart and to serve others around you humbly.

WEEK 20
DAY 5

I CAN SERVE OTHERS LIKE JESUS DID

Try This!

We often think that superheroes are important and proud. What do you think a humble superhero would look like? Design a cape with a logo for a humble hero.

I CAN SERVE OTHERS LIKE JESUS DID

WEEK 20
DAY 6

Try This!

Serving can be tough, especially around the house! Here's a guide to a few simple household chores. Choose one, and do it today. You are serving your family by doing this without complaining!

Laundry

1. Take a laundry basket and fill it with dirty clothes in your room.
2. Once you get to the laundry room, sort the clothes into LIGHT and DARK (ask a grown-up to help you sort).
3. Dump it into your washer and add detergent. You may need some help with this step!
4. Turn on the washer and wait for the clothes to be finished.
5. Once the clothes are done, place them in the dryer or on a clothes rack/line.
6. Once the clothes have dried, fold them and put them away! If you need help folding, ask a grown-up or older sibling to show you.

Sweeping

1. Grab a broom at your house and find an uncarpeted area.
2. Use the broom to sweep up the dirt around the house with a sweeping motion.
3. Once you've gotten most of the dirt, place the dustpan in front of the dirt and use the broom to sweep it into the dustpan!
4. Dump the dust into the garbage.

WEEK 21
DAY 1

I CAN TELL OTHERS ABOUT JESUS

> *Go into all the world and preach the Good News to everyone.*
>
> Mark 16:15

Read This!

Reid's pastor had challenged his church to tell at least one person they knew about Jesus.

As soon as Reid thought about telling others the story of Jesus, he got nervous. His stomach did flips, and his palms got all sweaty! He was just a kid. How was he supposed to tell others about Jesus?

As Reid walked in the door from school, he threw down his backpack and sat at the kitchen table. He turned to his mom and sighed, "Mom, how am I supposed to tell anyone the story of Jesus? I feel so nervous!"

His mom smiled. "Reid, all of us feel nervous when we have to tell others about Jesus! But, we can ask the Holy Spirit to help us. We were never meant to do it alone."

This made Reid feel a little better. His mom continued, "Plus, the Good News of Jesus and the super incredible things he has done for us is too good to keep to ourselves. We have to share it. Wouldn't you want someone to share the story with you?"

Reid nodded. What his mom was saying made sense! Even though he felt nervous, he knew that he could share the story of Jesus with a friend!

Fear Buster

I can share Jesus boldly, even when I feel scared, because I serve a super incredible God who gives me his super incredible power!

I CAN TELL OTHERS ABOUT JESUS

WEEK 21
DAY 2

Try This!

Create a poster that tells the story of Jesus. Use pictures and words, and let your creative juices flow! Once you're done, recreate it on a bigger piece of paper. Share the poster with a friend or family member who doesn't know Jesus.

WEEK 21
DAY 3

I CAN TELL OTHERS ABOUT JESUS

Try This!

Sometimes, when we are trying to tell a story, it helps to come up with some creative ways to remember it. In each of these six blocks, draw a symbol or small picture of ONE part of Jesus' story. Some parts of the story you might want to include are his birth, a miracle or teaching, the Last Supper, his death, or his resurrection.

I CAN TELL OTHERS ABOUT JESUS

WEEK 21
DAY 4

Go back to your family, and tell them everything God has done for you.

Luke 8:39

Read This!

Andi had just invited Jesus to be in charge of her life! Everything in her life seemed to be different since she had decided to follow Jesus.

Before she had known Jesus, she had been feeling very sad. Her family was always fighting, and her mom and dad were talking about splitting up. She felt like she was all alone.

One day, her friend Carter invited her to come along to a special event at his church. There, for the first time, she heard the story of Jesus, and that he had a super incredible love for her and the world.

On the drive home, she talked with Carter and his dad and asked them so many questions about Jesus and what it meant to follow him. As they pulled into her driveway, she made a decision. She whispered a prayer, telling Jesus she wanted him to be in charge of her life.

Andi was so thankful that Carter had been brave enough to tell her about Jesus and how Jesus had changed his life. Even though things were still bad at home, she knew that she could trust in Jesus to help her. She could even share the story of Jesus with her family and start praying for them, too!

Prayer Prompt

Who do you need to share the story of Jesus with? Pray and ask God to help you bravely share your story with others.

I CAN TELL OTHERS ABOUT JESUS

WEEK 21
DAY 5

Try This!

You may have heard of a testimony. A testimony is the story you share with others about the difference Jesus has made in your life. This simple sheet should help you write your very own testimony.

Why did you decide to follow Jesus? What was your life like before you started following him?

____

____

____

When did you start following Jesus?

____

How did it happen?

____

____

How is your life different now that you follow Jesus?

____

____

What is something super incredible that Jesus has done for you?

____

____

____

I CAN TELL OTHERS ABOUT JESUS

WEEK 21
DAY 6

Try This!

One of the ways many people tell their story is through art, including poems, raps, songs, dance routines, pictures, and more. On this page, come up with a creative way to tell the story of what Jesus has done in your life. You may want to write a poem or rap, write a song, create a dance routine, draw a picture, or something totally different. Whatever you choose, be sure to celebrate what Jesus has done for you!

WEEK 22 DAY 1

I SHOW OTHERS JESUS BY THE WAY I LIVE

> Don't copy the behavior and customs of this world, but let God transform you into a new person by changing the way you think.
>
> Romans 12:2

Read This!

If you've been following Jesus for a while, you will know that it's not always easy. Many of the things Jesus asks us to do—like be gentle, show love, or practice self-control—aren't easy or even common.

Many of your friends may choose not to follow Jesus, and their lives will look different than yours. While they may be kind or fun, they don't have the Holy Spirit working inside of them to make them more like Jesus.

The good news is that the way you live can show them Jesus and the love he has!

When you show patience, you are showing them that God is patient. When you choose to be kind to someone who doesn't deserve it, you show them that Jesus shows kindness. When you are gentle instead of mean, you show others that God is gentle.

The way you live may be different than those around you, but that's a good thing! It's a way that you can show others Jesus and the super incredible love he has for them.

Fear Buster

When I feel like I can't live for Jesus on my own, the Holy Spirit helps me live differently and show others his love!

I SHOW OTHERS JESUS BY THE WAY I LIVE

WEEK 22
DAY 2

Try This!

Let's write an acrostic poem! Using the word "DIFFERENT," write a poem describing the way Jesus followers should live.

D ______________________________

I ______________________________

F ______________________________

F ______________________________

E ______________________________

R ______________________________

E ______________________________

N ______________________________

T ______________________________

WEEK 22
DAY 3

I SHOW OTHERS JESUS BY THE WAY I LIVE

Try This!

Being different can be hard, but it can also be a good thing! Write about some ways you are different from those around you. How is that difficult? How is it good?

I SHOW OTHERS JESUS BY THE WAY I LIVE

WEEK 22
DAY 4

Let your good deeds shine out for all to see, so that everyone will praise your Heavenly Father.

Matthew 5:16

Read This!

Joshua watched as his classmate, Jessie, got more and more angry at the teacher.

"I don't know the answer!" Jessie, threw her paperback book at the teacher.

The teacher caught the book, but the class was in an uproar. Some were laughing, some were shocked, some gasped. But Joshua sat at his desk and watched his friend, Zack, bow his head. *Why does he keep doing that? Is he falling asleep?* Joshua wondered.

Joshua had noticed other strange things that Zack did. When Zack heard at school about kids on the other side of the globe who didn't have food to eat, he recruited his whole class to raise money for them!

Zack was kind to everyone, even to Jessie, the girl who nobody else talked to.

One day, Joshua had finally had enough! He had to ask Zack why he was so different. Zack just grinned and said: "I'm not that different than you, Joshua! The reason I do those things is because I want to show others the love of Jesus. He helps me live differently, and he can help you too!"

Prayer Prompt

Ask God to help you shine your light at school, at home, and with your friends!

WEEK 22
DAY 5

I SHOW OTHERS JESUS BY THE WAY I LIVE

Try This!

Have you ever made a shadow puppet? Tonight when you head to bed, or once it gets dark outside, grab a flashlight and turn off the lights in your room.

Place your hand in front of the flashlight, and make different shapes. Try animals, people, and faces. Just like the light shines in your dark room, you can shine for Jesus wherever you are!

I SHOW OTHERS JESUS BY THE WAY I LIVE

WEEK 22
DAY 6

Try This!

Inside this light bulb, you'll find all the letters you need for the words of Jesus in Matthew 5:16. Unscramble the letters and spell out the verse. Turn to the Bible if you need help!

L		T

D				

~~D~~ O ~~L~~ Y E N D U H G O D E E S O S E ~~T~~ I R

Answers on Page 318

WEEK 23
DAY 1

I CAN SHOW JESUS' LOVE TO MY FAMILY

> *Children, obey your parents because you belong to the Lord.*
> Ephesians 6:1

Read This!

Sitting on the desk in Julie's room was a super cool building set that she had gotten for her birthday last week. She had been so busy with school and after school sports that this was the first chance she would get to open the set and start building!

Just as Julie headed upstairs to open the set, her mom quietly said, "Hey, Julie, did you clean your room yet like I asked you to?" Julie cringed. She did not like cleaning her room, and she'd been putting it off.

Julie said nothing, and her mom continued, "I don't want you to do anything else until you get that room cleaned, OK?"

As she walked toward her room, Julie had to make a decision. Would she listen to her mom and start cleaning her room, or would she start playing anyway?

While she was trying to decide, Julie noticed her Bible lying on the desk. She was reminded of a verse she had learned at church a few weeks ago about obeying your parents. Obeying wasn't just showing love to her mom and dad—it was showing love to God as well!

Doing the right thing showed God she loved him, and it would show her mom, too.

Even though she didn't feel like it, Julie knew she needed to obey her mom and clean her room. She grabbed a cloth and a garbage bag and got to work. The building set could wait. And she would be pleasing God in the meantime!

Fear Buster

Sometimes, we don't want to obey our parents because we're scared we might miss out on something fun! God promises that when we obey our parents, he will bless us! There's no need to be scared of missing out when we follow God!

I CAN SHOW JESUS' LOVE TO MY FAMILY

WEEK 23
DAY 2

Try This!

On this page, draw a picture of your house! Include as many details as you'd like to. Inside, write ways you can obey your parents while you're at home. Remember, obeying doesn't just make them happy, it makes God happy, too!

WEEK 23
DAY 3

I CAN SHOW JESUS' LOVE TO MY FAMILY

Try This!

These might look like two ordinary stick figures, but your job is to transform them into your parents! Draw clothes, faces, and any other details that would make these stick figures look more like your parents. After you draw, write down three things you love about each of your parents!

I CAN SHOW JESUS' LOVE TO MY FAMILY

WEEK 23
DAY 4

May the LORD reward you for your kindness.

Ruth 1:8

Read This!

Ruth was still young when her husband got sick and died. She was so sad, but she knew her husband's mom, Naomi, was probably even sadder.

Ruth could still have a family and a future. Naomi, though, had lost her own husband and two sons to a horrible sickness. She felt all alone. Naomi decided that she was going to start the journey back to her home in Bethlehem to be close to her old friends and family.

Even though Ruth didn't have to, she decided to show kindness to Naomi. "Naomi shouldn't have to live and make the journey alone," Ruth thought. "I can show her God's love by traveling with her, staying with her, and helping her."

Naomi couldn't believe how kind Ruth was to her! Ruth kept working hard to show love to Naomi—to make sure she had food to eat, a place to sleep, and someone to keep her company. Ruth did this because she knew it was right. She did it because she wanted to show kindness to Naomi, and even more than that, show her God's love.

How can you be like Ruth, and show kindness to your family today?

Prayer Prompt

Thank God that he shows you kindness! Ask God to help you show kindness to the people in your family today.

WEEK 23
DAY 5

I CAN SHOW JESUS' LOVE TO MY FAMILY

Try This!

Ruth loved Naomi, even when it wasn't easy! We need to show love to our families too. With a parent's permission, find a family photo and stick it inside this Instagram frame. Create your very own hashtags beneath the picture to describe something great about your family.

• • •

33,530 likes

I CAN SHOW JESUS' LOVE TO MY FAMILY

WEEK 23
DAY 6

Try This!

Ruth was kind to Naomi in a lot of ways! On this piece of old-looking paper, write some ways you can follow her example and show kindness to your family.

WEEK 24
DAY 1

I CAN SHOW JESUS' LOVE TO MY FRIENDS

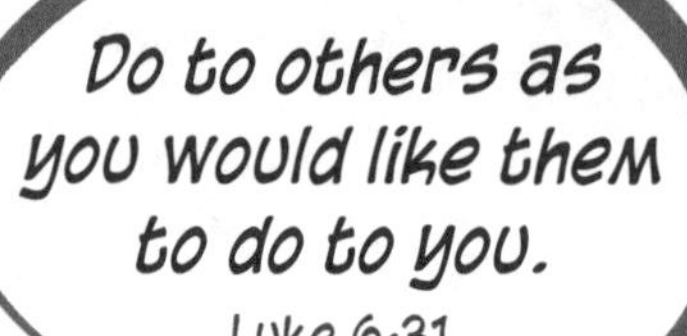

Read This!

"Hey Mason," Noah greeted his best friend at their lockers. "You're still coming over after school, right?"

Mason sighed, "I'm sorry, but I think I'd rather just go home after school."

Noah groaned, "Again? Mason, this is the third time this week that you've blown me off!"

Mason hunched his shoulders and stared at the ground. "Yeah, I'm sorry, I just want to be alone." Then he slung his backpack over his shoulder and walked away.

Noah clenched his jaw. *What a loser. I can't believe he canceled plans again!* He thought. *Why am I even friends with him, when it's clear he doesn't care about me?* Noah shoved his books into his backpack. *What's his problem anyway?*

Just then, Katie's locker swung open beside him. On the outside of the locker was a picture of her grandma who had recently passed away. Hadn't Mason mentioned something last week about his grandma getting sick? Noah thought for a moment. Mason had also mentioned that his parents had been fighting because they couldn't pay for his grandma's medical bills.

Noah zipped his backpack and swung it over his shoulder. Maybe Mason just needed a friend, even if he didn't show it. Noah knew that if he were going through a hard time like Mason, he would want someone to be kind to him, even if he didn't deserve it. Noah decided he would be extra kind to Mason the next time he saw him.

That's what Jesus would do, and Noah was trying to be more like Jesus every day!

Prayer Prompt

Think of some friends who you find it hard to be kind to sometimes. Ask God to give you patience to show them his love!

I CAN SHOW JESUS' LOVE TO MY FRIENDS

WEEK 24
DAY 2

Try This!

What kind of friend are you? Take this quiz to find out!

1. *If my friend is having a hard time with their homework, I*
   A. Tease them
   B. Let them copy my answers
   C. Ask the teacher to help
   D. Offer to help them
2. *My friends describe me as*
   A. Sarcastic, but funny
   B. Always trying to help
   C. Helpful when I want to be
   D. Dependable no matter what
3. *If my friend is feeling sad, I cheer them up by*
   A. Making fun of someone
   B. Giving them something
   C. Telling their mom and dad
   D. Spending time with them
4. *I tell my friends about Jesus*
   A. Never! We're always laughing.
   B. Even if they aren't interested
   C. I mostly leave it to grown-ups
   D. When it's a good opportunity

If you answered mostly *A*s, you are a funny friend! Being funny is a great trait to have, but make sure you look out for serious moments when they are needed.

If you answered mostly *B*s, you are a really helpful friend. You do whatever you can to help your friends, even if it's hard or maybe even wrong. Make sure that when you help them, you are asking God for help, too!

If you answered mostly *C*s, you are a safe friend! You are always making sure your friends are safe and helped by the people who love them. Make sure that you aren't so busy keeping your friends safe that you forget to be their friend! Sometimes they might just need you to be there for them.

If you answered mostly *D*s, you are a kind friend! You are trying to show your friends the love of Jesus! Keep up the good work, and show the love of Jesus as much as you can.

WEEK 24 DAY 3

I CAN SHOW JESUS' LOVE TO MY FRIENDS

Try This!

Friends are a great gift from God! On the trophies below, write the names of friends who are special to you. Beneath their trophies, write one way you can show that friend the love of Jesus!

I CAN SHOW JESUS' LOVE TO MY FRIENDS

WEEK 24
DAY 4

Two people are better off than one, for they can help each other succeed. If one person falls, the other can reach out and help.
Ecclesiastes 4:9-10

Read This!

Joey was feeling really bad for his friend Ben. For some reason, a few older boys at school had started bullying Ben. They made fun of his haircut, his clothes, and the way he talked. They were being mean to Ben, and Joey knew that his feelings were hurt.

Joey knew that he should keep being Ben's friend and even stand up for him. It was hard, though! What if he got made fun of, too? What if people started being mean to him? Sometimes, it was easier just to stay quiet.

As Joey thought about it, he remembered that part of being a good friend is sticking up for each other! Standing up for Ben even when it was hard would show Ben how much Joey loved him and how much Jesus loved him, too.

The next day, when the bullying started, Joey marched over, grabbed Ben by the arm, and brought him to another part of the playground. He told Ben that they could go on the monkey bars instead.

Joey saw the smile on Ben's face, and he knew that he was feeling better already. Being a friend that Ben could count on was a way to show Jesus' love!

Fear Buster

Sometimes, being a friend that people can count on means going into scary situations! God promises that when we do the right thing, he will be with us! We don't need to be scared.

WEEK 24
DAY 5

I CAN SHOW JESUS' LOVE TO MY FRIENDS

Try This!

It's important to be a friend that people can count on! But how good are you at just regular counting? Use this code to figure out an important message from the Bible on friendship. Look up Proverbs 17:17 if you need help!

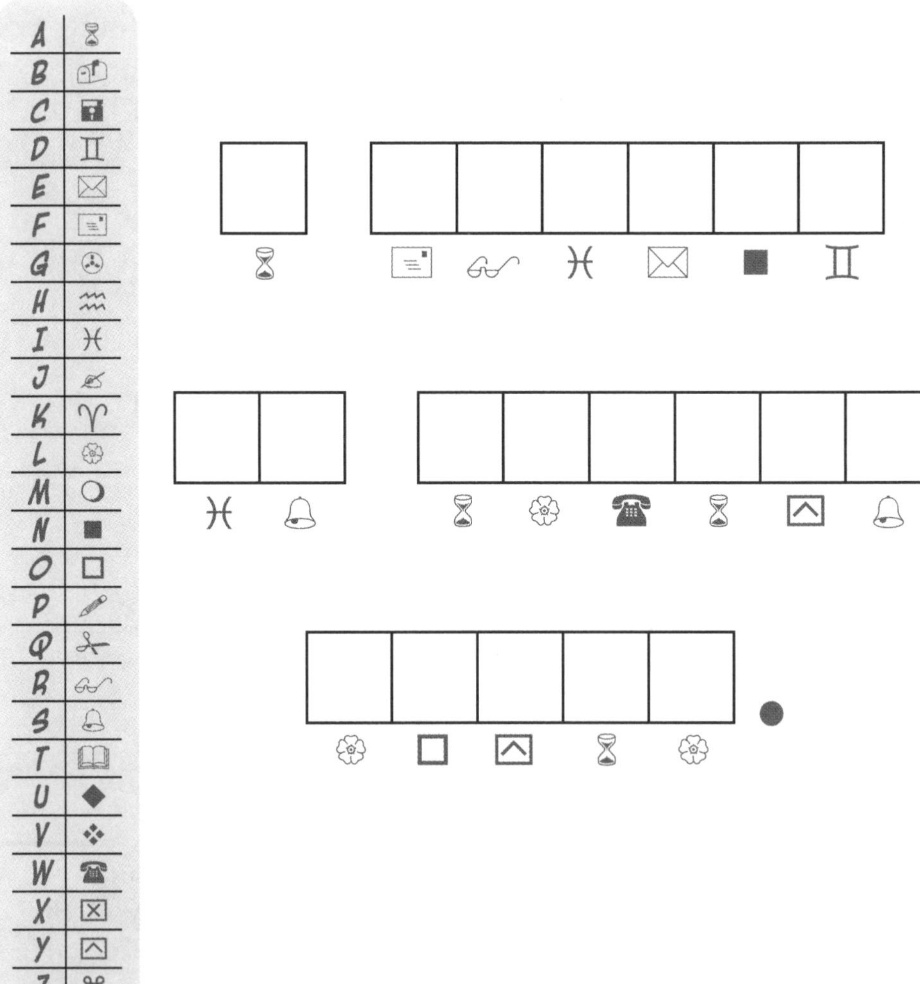

Answers on Page 318

Try This!

What makes a good friend? Fill in these letters with words that describe a good friend. Bonus if you only use words that start with each letter!

F ______________________________

R ______________________________

I ______________________________

E ______________________________

N ______________________________

D ______________________________

WEEK 25

DAY 1

I CAN LOVE PEOPLE WHO HURT ME

> Love your enemies! Do good to those who hate you. Bless those who curse you. Pray for those who hurt you.
>
> Luke 6:27-28

Read This!

Sometimes, people are just plain mean. They make fun of us, they say mean things, and they really hurt our feelings.

In those times, we have a choice to make. We can choose to be mean back to them, hurting them with our words or actions. We can choose to hate them and not let them have a part of our hearts. We can choose to get bitter and angry.

Or, we can choose to show Jesus' love.

That doesn't mean we let people walk all over us, but it does mean that we choose to respond with kindness instead of being mean. It means that we forgive them, even when they don't deserve it. And, we choose to keep our hearts soft and ready to love.

Loving those who hurt us isn't easy! But it's what Jesus would do. And with his help, we can do it, too!

Prayer Prompt

Ask God to help you forgive the people who hurt you, and show them his love.

I CAN LOVE PEOPLE WHO HURT ME

WEEK 25
DAY 2

Try This!

Draw a comic strip of how you can respond the next time someone hurts you! Think about what Jesus would do. Use speech bubbles and cartoon drawings!

WEEK 25
DAY 3

I CAN LOVE PEOPLE WHO HURT ME

Try This!

Forgiving people who are mean to us is a hard thing to do! Write a letter to someone who has hurt you, telling them you forgive them. When you are done, pray and ask God to help you keep showing his love to that person.

I CAN LOVE PEOPLE WHO HURT ME

WEEK 25
DAY 4

Even if you suffer for doing what is right, God will reward you for it.

1 Peter 3:14

Read This!

Jenna was tired of constantly being made fun of for following Jesus.

It seemed like every day at school kids were saying something about her decision to follow Jesus.

"You're such a goody two-shoes, Jenna!"

"Why do you care about church so much?"

"God isn't real, why would you waste your time?"

As hard as she tried to stay strong, there were days she just felt like crying. Was following Jesus really worth it? Did she have to be nice to those people?

One night, as Jenna read her Bible, she read words from Jesus. He said that people would be mean to us when we follow him, but we should stand strong. He even said we should show them his love.

That sounded hard!

Jenna knew that she wanted to follow Jesus and show his love to others. Even though it still hurt her feelings, she would try to show God's love to those who made fun of her. Who knows? Maybe someday they would come to know Jesus, too!

Fear Buster

It can be scary to think about being made fun of for following Jesus! Thankfully, Jesus promised that his super incredible Holy Spirit would be with us every step of the way.

I CAN LOVE PEOPLE WHO HURT ME

Try This!

Sometimes, following Jesus can be scary and confusing, especially when people make fun of us! Thankfully, we have a guide in God. Make your way through this maze. On the blank lines, print the words you find along the way.

____

____

____

____

Answers on Page 319

I CAN LOVE PEOPLE WHO HURT ME

WEEK 25
DAY 6

Try This!

Jesus tells us to be kind and show love to people who make fun of us! Brainstorm some ways you can show kindness to the people who make fun of you or are mean. Some ideas might be:

- *Make a card*
- *Bake them something*
- *Make them a craft*
- *Write them a note*

Brainstorm some ideas below—you can write, draw, and plan as much as needed—and then with permission from a grown-up, go ahead and do it! Show them God's love even when it's hard!

WEEK 26
DAY 1

I CAN SHOW JESUS' LOVE TO AUTHORITY

> *Pray this way for kings and all who are in authority so that we can live peaceful and quiet lives marked by godliness and dignity. This is good and pleases God our Savior.*
>
> 1 Timothy 2:2-3

Read This!

Kristen's mom didn't let her watch the news very often, but she overheard her parents, teachers, and friends all talking about it! It seemed like every day people were talking about the government, the mayor, and all the trouble they were facing.

Kristen didn't know much about how the government or city council worked, but she knew their job must be tough! They had to make hard decisions every single day. They were always on the news, being interviewed. People had tons of opinions about them.

She didn't know what she could do to show those people God's love, but she knew they needed it to. One Sunday at church, she asked her pastor about it. Her pastor showed her a verse in 1 Timothy that talked about praying for the people who were in authority.

Kristen might not be able to do much, but she could do that! She decided that each night, before she went to bed, she would say a prayer for the people in charge of her town and her country. She prayed that God would help them and show them his love. Maybe her little prayer would make a big difference.

Prayer Prompt

Take some time today to pray for the people that lead your town, state/province, or country! Ask God to guide them and show them his love.

I CAN SHOW JESUS' LOVE TO AUTHORITY

WEEK 26
DAY 2

Try This!

If you were in charge of a country, what would the flag look like? In this blank flag, design your perfect one! Draw and color. Come up a name for your country, and write it below the flag. Once you've completed that, take a minute to pray for some countries around the world!

I CAN SHOW JESUS' LOVE TO AUTHORITY

Try This!

Make a list of all the people you know who are in government. You may need to use the internet or a grown-up to help you. Include people in your local town, state or province, and country! Write down their names on this sheet, and then stick it up somewhere you will see it! This will help you remember to pray for them.

I CAN SHOW JESUS' LOVE TO AUTHORITY

WEEK 26
DAY 4

So you must submit to them, not only to avoid punishment, but also to keep a clear conscience.

Romans 13:5

Read This!

As kids, it can be hard to understand people in charge.

- Our parents and their rules don't always make sense to us!
- Our teachers seem like they don't want us to have any fun.
- The people who make laws seem strict and scary.

Does the Bible have anything to say about how we are supposed to treat people in charge? Actually, it does! The Bible makes clear that we are supposed to show respect to the people who are in charge of us. Whether parents, teachers, babysitters, pastors, or the government, God wants us to listen to them and show them respect.

Showing them respect is a way of showing God our love! You see, God is the one who gives them the ability to be in charge in the first place! When we respect them, we are saying "God, we respect you, too!"

That doesn't mean it's always easy, and it doesn't mean we will always want to! What it does mean is that when we do listen, respect, and love those in charge, we are showing God love.

And that is what super incredible faith is all about!

Fear Buster

Sometimes, people who are in charge can seem strict or mean. If we trust God, he will protect us as we show respect and listen to him.

WEEK 26
DAY 5

I CAN SHOW JESUS' LOVE TO AUTHORITY

Try This!

Draw pictures of three people you respect. Write a couple sentences for each of them about why you respect them.

I CAN SHOW JESUS' LOVE TO AUTHORITY

WEEK 26
DAY 6

Try This!

Write a letter to someone who is in charge. This could be a parent, teacher, pastor, or someone else. Tell them three things you like about them and that you are praying for them. Give them the letter the next time you see them!

WEEK 27
DAY 1

I CAN LOVE PEOPLE WHO ARE DIFFERENT THAN ME

Read This!

> My dear brothers and sisters, how can you claim to have faith in our glorious Lord Jesus Christ if you favor some people over others?
>
> James 2:1

Chloe's class at school was full of kids from all over the world! At her table sat Jason, who had just moved to her state from Canada. Across the room was Jendayi, whose family was originally from Zimbabwe.

In the cafeteria, she passed by Ahmed, who had just arrived from the Middle East. He was still learning English, and a lot of kids made fun of his accent and the clothes he wore.

Chloe had to be honest. Sometimes it was hard to accept people who were different. She wasn't used to the way that they looked, talked, or even the food they ate. Sometimes, the easiest thing to do was laugh at something she didn't understand.

But she knew that Jesus wouldn't do that. In fact, last week at church, her pastor had talked about how God accepted people from all over the world into his family. Heaven would be a place that showed off how different God's great family was! If Jesus loved and made all these people, Chloe knew she should love them, too.

She turned around in the cafeteria and plopped down next to Ahmed. Other people could make fun of her if they wanted. She knew Jesus was on her side, and she was living out his super incredible love!

Fear Buster

Sometimes, people or things that are different can make us feel nervous or uncomfortable. We can trust that our super incredible God is looking out for us, and he made people different to show his creativity and love!

Try This!

On this map of the world, put a star or another symbol on the countries that you know somebody from. Isn't it amazing that God made every person and country differently?

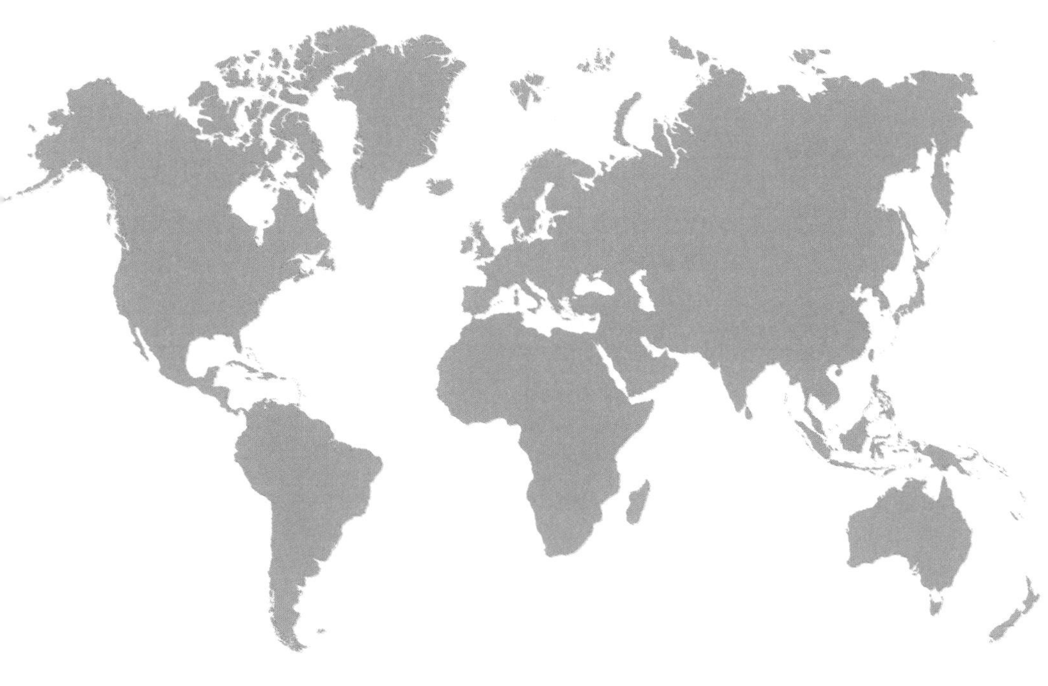

I CAN LOVE PEOPLE WHO ARE DIFFERENT THAN ME

Try This!

Pick one of these countries, and with the help or permission of a grown-up, find out some facts about it! Celebrate what makes that country different than yours.

MEXICO
INDIA
PHILIPPINES
AUSTRALIA
CHINA
GERMANY
SOUTH AFRICA

Name of Country: ______________________________

Language Spoken: ______________________________

Population: ______________________________

Draw a picture of their flag:

What do they eat there? ______________________________

____

What's the weather like? ______________________________

____

What do they do for fun? ______________________________

____

I CAN LOVE PEOPLE WHO ARE DIFFERENT THAN ME

WEEK 27
DAY 4

There are different kinds of service, but we serve the same Lord. God works in different ways, but it is the same God who does the work in all of us.
1 Corinthians 12:5-6

Read This!

"Mom, can you tell Katie to stop complaining about setting up for VBS?" Lucas asked one evening. He was sitting at the table cutting out starfish and crab shapes for their VBS theme.

Lucas absolutely loved helping out with VBS decorating. This year he was finally old enough to tag along. He had been cutting, painting, and tracing decorations for a few days now. But his older sister, Katie, was no fun to work with.

"What is she complaining about?" Mom asked as she washed the dishes.

"Everything! She doesn't want to paint or cut or tape or anything!" Lucas explained, "At church today she kept asking to organize papers at the welcome desk. How boring is that? Who would choose organization over painting?"

Mom smiled to herself. "That's not complaining," she laughed. "It's just that you two have different interests. God made us all different. We have different gifts and talents, likes and dislikes, and personalities. That's what makes life interesting and exciting. You like to be creative and Katie likes to organize. Both are great gifts. We couldn't get everything ready for VBS if we all did the same job."

Lucas thought for a moment. He knew he had to accept Katie and thank God for her super incredible talents, even when they were different than his!

Prayer Prompt

Thank God for at least four people who do things differently than you! Celebrate how he makes us all different.

I CAN LOVE PEOPLE WHO ARE DIFFERENT THAN ME

Try This!

Inside the first gift box, make a list of all the things that you are good at or like doing! In the second gift box, ask some of your friends and family the things they like doing. Then compare. Which ones are the same? Which ones are different? Thank God that he uses everyone for his kingdom!

I CAN LOVE PEOPLE WHO ARE DIFFERENT THAN ME

WEEK 27
DAY 6

Try This!

Find the words of our verse in this word search! Once you've found all the words, put them in verse order!

F	X	J	L	N	A	R	S	A	E	C	C	P	H	A	J	S	X
I	M	A	M	T	V	O	D	E	O	W	Y	E	U	B	O	P	A
C	B	P	T	H	D	Y	I	Z	R	X	R	S	Y	G	H	J	O
X	Q	X	T	J	Q	K	F	D	B	V	A	V	F	F	B	A	A
B	S	H	G	H	Y	J	F	R	Y	P	I	L	Z	A	W	C	P
V	H	A	C	F	C	G	E	J	V	M	W	C	V	G	C	M	M
M	K	S	M	L	T	Z	R	W	K	T	L	X	E	K	F	S	B
I	L	E	Y	E	S	N	E	W	V	I	E	G	N	G	Z	E	N
W	C	O	G	C	G	W	N	Q	P	C	N	B	I	H	V	R	N
F	I	L	R	O	Y	R	T	L	M	H	T	D	Y	B	T	V	R
S	D	T	L	D	U	H	M	N	R	K	O	R	S	C	N	E	L
M	D	Q	K	B	I	H	J	S	X	E	Q	W	I	U	B	I	Q

Different   Service   Same
Kinds   Serve   Lord

Answers on Page 319

PAUL SHARED JESUS WITH OTHERS

WEEK 28
DAY 1

Read This!

> The Lord said, "Go, for Saul is my chosen instrument to take my message to the Gentiles and to kings, as well as to the people of Israel."
>
> Acts 9:15

Have you ever met a bully? Paul, previously known as Saul, was the worst bully you could possibly imagine. His whole job was bullying Jesus followers.

He spent his days traveling from town to town hunting down Christians, arresting them, and even having them killed! He was proud of his work. He thought these Christians were crazy!

One day, everything changed for Paul. While on his way to capture more Christians, Jesus showed up! With bright lights and a loud voice, he stopped Paul on the road and asked Paul to start following him!

Everything changed for Paul in that moment. Instead of hunting down Christians, he worked to make as many people Christians as possible. He traveled around the world sharing the good news of Jesus, preaching, teaching, and doing miracles.

God had a super incredible purpose for Paul's life, and Paul was willing to say "Yes!" What super incredible things does God want you to do?

Fear Buster

Can you imagine how scared Paul must have been when he met Jesus for the first time? Sometimes, when God calls us to do things, it can be scary! Thankfully, he promises to be with us no matter what!

PAUL SHARED JESUS WITH OTHERS

WEEK 28
DAY 2

Try This!

Draw a comic strip about Paul's story. Check out Acts 9 in your Bible to help you!

WEEK 28 DAY 3

PAUL SHARED JESUS WITH OTHERS

Try This!

Make a wanted poster for Paul describing his life change. Draw his picture and describe the change that happened to Paul when he met Jesus.

PAUL SHARED JESUS WITH OTHERS

WEEK 28
DAY 4

How will anyone go and tell them without being sent? That is why the Scriptures say, "How beautiful are the feet of messengers who bring good news!"

Romans 10:15

Read This!

After Paul met Jesus, things changed in his life! He started preaching about Jesus everywhere he went. He preached in temples and he preached in the streets.

He shared Jesus with the Jews, who knew about God, and the Gentiles, who had not yet heard about Jesus!

Paul traveled to cities and churches all around his part of the world, telling people about Jesus. He wrote about Jesus, too, and many of his letters are a part of the Bible today.

Even when he faced opposition—from people trying to kill him to his ship being wrecked—he didn't stop telling people about Jesus!

Paul believed that God had chosen him to preach the good news about Jesus, and he wouldn't let anything stop him! He wanted everyone to know the super incredible news about Jesus, and would do anything to share that news!

How can you be like Paul and share the super incredible news about Jesus with people around you?

Prayer Prompt

Pray and ask God to give you courage to share the good news about Jesus with people in your life!

PAUL SHARED JESUS WITH OTHERS

Try This!

Paul said that feet that travel to preach the good news of Jesus are beautiful. Trace an outline of your foot on this page, then decorate it to make it as beautiful as possible. As you do, think about how you can share Jesus' good news!

PAUL SHARED JESUS WITH OTHERS

WEEK 28
DAY 6

Try This!

You may not have to go around the world to tell people about Jesus. There are probably people you can tell about Jesus close by! Make a list of people you know who need to know about Jesus, and where you can find them!

WEEK 29
DAY 1

PETER BROUGHT JESUS TO PEOPLE FAR FROM GOD

> *Peter stepped forward with the eleven other apostles and shouted to the crowd.*
> Acts 2:14

Read This!

Peter was one of Jesus' best friends. He was with Jesus when he performed miracles, fed thousands of people, and preached the good news that God's kingdom was here!

He was also there when Jesus died on the cross, even though he lied about knowing Jesus.

Jesus forgave Peter for his mistake, and Peter saw Jesus when he rose from the dead. God gave Peter a special job to "feed his sheep," or to take care of God's people.

After Jesus had returned to Heaven, Peter and Jesus' other followers received God's power through the Holy Spirit. People were confused about what was happening, so Peter stood up and preached to a humongous crowd! He told them the story of Jesus and how he could save anyone and everyone. After they heard Peter's message, three thousand people decided to follow Jesus!

Wow! Peter, an ordinary guy, did a super incredible thing when he trusted in God! God used him to reach thousands of people with the good news of Jesus. This was just the beginning of Peter's story. God had an amazing plan for his life!

Fear Buster

Sometimes, when we make mistakes (like Peter did), we think God won't use us! Thankfully, we can trust that God loves us and uses us even when we make mistakes!

PETER BROUGHT JESUS TO PEOPLE FAR FROM GOD

WEEK 29
DAY 2

Try This!

Imagine the scene of Peter preaching in Acts 2! Now draw it! Include a speech bubble with some of the words you think he may have said! You can check out Acts 2 if you're not sure.

WEEK 29
DAY 3

PETER BROUGHT JESUS TO PEOPLE FAR FROM GOD

Try This!

Imagine that you are Peter, and have to preach a sermon about Jesus to a huge crowd of people! Use the space below to write what you would say. After you're done, practice delivering your sermon to family or friends!

PETER BROUGHT JESUS TO PEOPLE FAR FROM GOD

WEEK 29

DAY 4

I see very clearly that God shows no favoritism. In every nation he accepts those who fear him and do what is right.

Acts 10:34-35

Read This!

After Peter preached his super incredible sermon to the crowd, he continued to tell people about Jesus! He talked about him on the streets and in the temple.

There was one thing though—Peter only told Jews, God's chosen people, about Jesus. He didn't tell strangers or people from other countries.

One day, God showed up in a special dream to Peter. God talked to Peter and told him to search for the house of Cornelius. Cornelius was a man from another country who wanted to know about Jesus.

Peter was confused—could people who weren't Jews know about Jesus, too?

Peter could have said no to telling Cornelius and his family about Jesus, but he didn't. He trusted that God wanted everyone to know the good news about Jesus, and it was his incredible job to tell them!

Because Peter listened to God, many people from all over the world came to know Jesus. When we trust God, he uses us for his super incredible plans. How can you listen to God and share Jesus with people who may be far away from him?

Prayer Prompt

Are there people who are different than you who need to know about Jesus? Pray that God would give you courage to share his love with them!

WEEK 29
DAY 5

PETER BROUGHT JESUS TO PEOPLE FAR FROM GOD

Try This!

Look up Acts 10 in your Bible. Read the story of Peter sharing the good news about Jesus to Cornelius. Then, create a script for a play to act it out! If you're really brave, act it out for someone in your house!

PETER BROUGHT JESUS TO PEOPLE FAR FROM GOD

WEEK 29
DAY 6

Try This!

It's time for a super incredible scavenger hunt! Search for these items around your home. As you look, think of what it might have been like for Peter to search for Cornelius. Once you're done, try hiding these same objects in different places and have a family member or friend find them. You can even lead them along the way like Peter was led by God to Cornelius! Write down where you hid each item below so they don't get lost!

PAPER CLIP ______________________

YELLOW BOOK ______________________

NICKEL ______________________

SNACK FOOD ______________________

FUN SOCKS ______________________

PEN WITH BLUE INK ______________________

HEADPHONES/EARBUDS ______________________

COFFEE MUG ______________________

LIP BALM ______________________

RED MARKER ______________________

WEEK 30 DAY 1

LYDIA HELPED FOLLOWERS OF JESUS

Read This!

One of them was Lydia from Thyatira, a merchant of expensive purple cloth, who worshiped God. As she listened to us, the Lord opened her heart, and she accepted what Paul was saying.

Acts 16:14

Lydia had sat beside the river praying. She came here every day around the same time. Some of her friends came with her, and they sat and prayed. They talked about God, if he was real, what he was like, and how they could get to know him.

They had a lot of questions but not a lot of answers. Still, they knew they wanted to follow Jesus.

One day, a strange man came and sat down at the river near them. He had a group of other men with him. They seemed different than other men Lydia had met— kinder, happier, and braver. They started telling Lydia and the other women about the God they prayed to.

Soon, they started to talk about a man named Jesus, about his life, his death, and how he was raised from the tomb. They talked about how he could take away sins.

Lydia's heart began to race. This is what she had been waiting to hear! God had heard her prayers! He was showing her and her friends that he was real.

Lydia knew what she had to do. She needed to trust this super incredible God and start living her life for him. All the money that she had, all the friends she had made, none of that mattered. All that mattered was following Jesus and loving him with her whole heart!

Prayer Prompt

Maybe you are like Lydia and you have questions about God! Pray and ask God to show you more of Jesus and help you trust him more!

LYDIA HELPED FOLLOWERS OF JESUS

WEEK 30
DAY 2

Try This!

Lydia was a "dealer of purple cloth." She dyed and sold beautiful purple cloth to people in the city! Make this purple play dough from scratch to remind you of Lydia and her business!

Materials

- 2 ½ cup flour, sifted
- ½ cup salt
- 3 tablespoons cooking oil
- 1 or 2 packages unsweetened grape-flavored soft drink mix
- 1 cup very hot water

Directions

1. Mix together flour, salt, oil, and drink mix.
2. Add the cup of almost boiling water. Mix well.
3. Knead the mixture until it forms a soft dough.

WEEK 30
DAY 3

LYDIA HELPED FOLLOWERS OF JESUS

Try This!

Lydia and her friends sat by the river praying and talking about God! Make a poster advertising their meetings that they may have posted around their city. How do you think their poster would have changed after Paul came to preach?

LYDIA HELPED FOLLOWERS OF JESUS

WEEK 30
DAY 4

[Lydia] and her household were baptized, and she asked us to be her guests. "If you agree that I am a true believer in the Lord," she said, "come and stay at my home."
Acts 16:15

Read This!

Lydia was a wealthy business woman in her city. Her business of selling purple cloth may seem silly to us today, but in her time, it was a very important business. She made lots of money from selling this cloth to people who were rich and royal!

No one knows what Lydia did with all her money before she met Jesus. She may have given some to the poor. She may have used it to buy nice, new things. Maybe she used it all for more purple cloth!

When she heard the message of Jesus, she knew she needed to live differently! Right away, Lydia invited Paul and his friends to stay at her house. She could use what she had to help them as they told others about Jesus! They stayed at her house, and she helped support them with money, food, and friendship as they told others about Jesus.

Lydia could have kept her things and her house to herself, but instead, she decided to use them to help God's people! How can you be like Lydia and use what you have to help others?

Fear Buster

Sometimes, we want to keep all the good things we have to ourselves. We're afraid by sharing, we will run out! Lydia's story is a reminder that God gives us good things to share, and he always takes care of us!

WEEK 30
DAY 5

LYDIA HELPED FOLLOWERS OF JESUS

Try This!

Lydia invited Paul and his friends to stay at her house. What do you think her house would have looked like? What was it like outside, and what do you think was inside? Draw what you think Lydia's house may have looked like.

LYDIA HELPED FOLLOWERS OF JESUS

WEEK 30
DAY 6

Try This!

How can you use what you have to help those who follow Jesus? Fill in the blanks.

One thing I can do with my time to help others is:

____

____

One thing I can buy with my money to serve Jesus is:

____

____

One thing I can give to other followers of Jesus is:

____

____

One thing I should share with other followers of Jesus:

____

____

I can be like Lydia by:

____

____

PRISCILLA AND AQUILA TAUGHT ABOUT JESUS

WEEK 31
DAY 1

Read This!

> When Priscilla and Aquila heard him preaching boldly in the synagogue, they took him aside and explained the way of God even more accurately.
>
> Acts 18:26

Apollos was a new Christian. He had just started learning about Jesus, and was great at telling others about him! He traveled frequently, telling others the good news about Jesus.

On his travels, he arrived at a city called Ephesus. Once he was there, he went to the temple and told the people there all about Jesus!

Even though Apollos loved Jesus, there were still some things he didn't know. He was still learning, after all. But it wasn't good for him to be misleading people about the truth. Thankfully, two Jesus-followers in Ephesus were willing to help him.

Aquila and Priscilla were a husband and wife who loved Jesus and loved teaching! When they heard Apollos teaching, they invited him to their home. While he was there, they told him more about Jesus and helped him become the best teacher about Jesus he could be! They shared their super incredible faith with him and with others too!

Fear Buster

Sometimes, teaching others can be scary! Maybe we'd rather keep quiet! God promises he will be with us and even give us the right words to say when we are talking about him.

PRISCILLA AND AQUILA TAUGHT ABOUT JESUS

WEEK 31
DAY 2

Try This!

If you could ask Aquila and Priscilla any question about Jesus, what would it be? Write it down here, and then write out how they might answer!

WEEK 31
DAY 3

PRISCILLA AND AQUILA TAUGHT ABOUT JESUS

Try This!

Make a list of things you know about Jesus that you could teach to someone else. Maybe it's a friend who just got to know Jesus, a younger kid at church, or a brother or sister.

1.

2.

3.

4.

5.

6.

7.

8.

9.

10.

PRISCILLA AND AQUILA TAUGHT ABOUT JESUS

WEEK 31
DAY 4

Give my greetings to Priscilla and Aquila, my co-workers in the ministry of Christ Jesus.

Romans 16:3

Read This!

Sometimes, we think that being a hero means doing really exciting things.

- Maybe we will get to stand in front of a crowd and shout "Jesus saves!"
- Maybe we will get to rescue someone who's hurting.
- Maybe God will use us to go to another country and help people who need him.

While sometimes that's what being a hero looks like, sometimes it doesn't! Priscilla and Aquila were heroes of the faith, even when they didn't get to do exciting things. A lot of Priscilla and Aquila's life was spent helping other heroes.

They spent their time giving money, making tents to support other Christians, and teaching others about Jesus. They let other people, like Paul, stay in the spotlight while they worked quietly in the background.

To other people, they may not have seemed super incredible. They probably just seemed like boring, ordinary Jesus followers. But they were so much more than that! They were following Jesus on a super incredible faith adventure. They knew that God had a plan for them, and they were doing their best to follow it. That's what being a super incredible hero for Jesus is all about!

Prayer Prompt

How does God want you to be a hero? Pray and ask him to guide you and help you do what he asks.

WEEK 31 DAY 5

PRISCILLA AND AQUILA TAUGHT ABOUT JESUS

Try This!

Sometimes, helping is not very fun! On this page, write a song, poem or rap that you can sing or say when you're doing things that are hard or not fun. Make sure to mention that you're serving Jesus while you help in your creation!

PRISCILLA AND AQUILA TAUGHT ABOUT JESUS

WEEK 31
DAY 6

Try This!

Did you know that Aquila and Priscilla made tents when they weren't helping others serve Jesus? Grab some blankets and chairs at your house, and make a tent! While you're in there, read Acts 18 to hear the whole story of Aquila and Priscilla.

WEEK 32
DAY 1
FOLLOWERS OF JESUS MEET AT CHURCH

Read This!

> All the believers met together in one place and shared everything they had.
>
> Acts 2:44

Can you imagine what it would have been like to be a Christian thousands of years ago?

There weren't a lot of people who were following Jesus yet, and there were no nice church buildings to meet in. They didn't have worship bands with guitars and drums. There was no children's church!

Instead, those first followers of Jesus met in each other's homes. They gathered to sing, pray, and read the Bible. They ate together, talked to each other, and shared everything they had.

Those first Christians set an example for us thousands of years later! They knew that meeting together was important, whether at a house or a church. They needed each other to grow stronger as followers of Jesus and to learn more about him. They helped each other in hard times and loved each other in good times.

When we go to church, we are part of something that has been happening for thousands of years! We are honoring our super incredible God, and we're part of a super incredible legacy!

Fear Buster

Sometimes we can feel nervous about going to a new place like church! If you feel scared about going to church, you can trust that God is with you and that church was his idea in the first place!

FOLLOWERS OF JESUS MEET AT CHURCH

WEEK 32
DAY 2

Try This!

Here's a picture of a house church from thousands of years ago! Draw people outside doing the different things described in Acts 2.

WEEK 32
DAY 3

FOLLOWERS OF JESUS MEET AT CHURCH

Try This!

Extra! Extra, read all about it! The first church meeting is happening in Jerusalem this week! Draw a picture, headline, and some information about that first meeting. What do you think the Jerusalem news would be reporting?

Current Press

DAILY NEWS

All news in one newspaper

Issue: 240460

FOLLOWERS OF JESUS MEET AT CHURCH

WEEK 32
DAY 4

Let us not neglect our meeting together, as some people do, but encourage one another, especially now that the day of his return is drawing near.

Hebrews 10:25

Read This!

"Why do we have to go to church anyway?" Tessa yelled at her mom one Sunday morning. Mom ignored the question and tried to hand Tessa her shoes.

Tessa crossed her arms over her chest. "I hate going to church. It's so boring. We always sing the same songs and none of my school friends have to go. Skye and Jordan play games on Sunday morning or they ride their bikes to the park. Why can't we do that?"

Mom put the shoes down. "You can ride your bike to church if you want," she smiled. Church was at least a twenty-minute car ride. Tessa groaned. There was no way Tessa was doing that.

Mom sat down on the couch and opened the Bible on the coffee table. "You know church wasn't my idea. It was God's." She opened to the book of Hebrews. "It wasn't just for singing or for social time. It was a place for Christians to meet with God and with each other."

"Church was meant to be a place where people could go to be encouraged when they were having bad days. It was meant to be a place they could celebrate when they were having good days! And, it was meant to be a place people went to no matter if they felt like it or not."

Even though Tessa still didn't really feel like going, she understood that church was important to being a follower of Jesus.

Prayer Prompt

Thank God for the church you go to or ask him to help you and your family find a church home.

WEEK 32
DAY 5

FOLLOWERS OF JESUS MEET AT CHURCH

Try This!

Make a list of FIVE things you love about your church!
Share them with your pastor or kids' leader.

MY TOP 5!

1.

2.

3.

4.

5.

FOLLOWERS OF JESUS MEET AT CHURCH

WEEK 32
DAY 6

Try This!

Design an invitation that you could give to someone who was going to church for the first time. What would they need to know? Include it on your invite!

You're Invited!

WEEK 33
DAY 1

I CAN GROW IN FAITH AT CHURCH

Read This!

Their responsibility is to equip God's people to do his work and build up the church, the body of Christ.

Ephesians 4:12

Terrence was a world-famous body builder. He could lift hundreds of pounds and it seemed like he was made of muscle! Some people whispered that they thought Terrence was so strong that he could move a truck all by himself.

Terrence was strong, but he hadn't always been that way. Growing up, Terrence didn't have any muscles. He didn't like exercising or eating healthy food. He couldn't imagine being strong, let alone a body builder!

One day, some of Terrence's friends started lifting weights. He tagged along, and before he knew it, he was lifting weights, too! Those friends started eating healthy, and so did he. Soon enough, he was growing muscles and getting spiritually stronger every day. He couldn't believe how strong he was now, but he couldn't have done it without the help of his friends.

Just like Terrence's friends helped him grow physically stronger, going to church helps us grow spiritually stronger, too! When we meet with God's family, we can hear God's Word, pray for each other, and worship God together. When we are feeling weak, God's family can help us grow stronger. We are blessed to have such a super incredible family in the church!

Prayer Prompt

Thank God for your church family who can help you grow stronger. Pray for people in your church who may need God's strength right now.

Try This!

How strong are you? One of the easiest ways to find out how strong you are is to do a plank challenge!

Get down on the floor and lift yourself up on your arms! Keep your body straight from your back to your heels, and get up on you tiptoes. You should form a straight line. See how long you can hold the plank and record it here.

Try this activity with some other friends and family members and record their times, too. Who's the strongest one in your house?

WEEK 33
DAY 3

I CAN GROW IN FAITH AT CHURCH

Try This!

God gave us the church to help build us stronger in faith. Rate these things in order from least strong (1) to most strong (5)! When you're done, thank God that no matter how strong or weak you may feel, the people in your church family can help you stay strong in your relationship with Jesus.

1 - 2 - 3 - 4 - 5

1 - 2 - 3 - 4 - 5

1 - 2 - 3 - 4 - 5

1 - 2 - 3 - 4 - 5

I CAN GROW IN FAITH AT CHURCH

WEEK 33
DAY 4

So encourage each other and build each other up, just as you are already doing.
1 Thessalonians 5:11

Read This!

Tiffany was having a hard week. It seemed like nothing was going right! She had gotten a bad mark on her math assignment, and then her teacher yelled at her for talking.

She and her sister had gotten into a giant fight on Saturday morning over something silly. It left her feeling bad.

When she got to church on Sunday, she just wasn't feeling good about anything. She felt down about herself, her family, and her grades. Honestly, Tiffany didn't want to talk to or see anybody.

Something amazing happened when she got to church though! As her pastor was speaking, she started to feel God's peace in her heart. As the worship team sang, she remembered how much God loved her. When her small group leader prayed for her, she felt like God actually cared.

Even though Tiffany's life hadn't changed, going to church reminded her how important her relationship with Jesus was. Even when things were hard, she needed to trust in Jesus to be her help and to hold on to him. She was so glad she had went to church, or she may have forgotten how super incredible God is!

Fear Buster

Sometimes, we can be scared of what life throws at us! God gave us the church to help us grow closer to him during hard times!

WEEK 33
DAY 5

I CAN GROW IN FAITH AT CHURCH

Try This!

Make a list of different people who help others grow closer to Jesus in your church! Include their names as well as their positions. Here are some ideas to get you started:

Pastor
Worship Leader
Children's Pastor
Greeter
Small Group Leader
Usher

Try This!

How can you encourage someone in your church today? Maybe making this simple cereal-cookie recipe for them would be an encouragement! Make a note or card saying how much you care about them to go with it.

Ingredients

- 5 cups crispy rice cereal
- 4 cups mini marshmallows
- ¼ cup butter

Directions

1. Melt butter in large sauce pan over low heat.
2. Add marshmallows and stir until melted and well-blended. Cook 2 minutes longer, stirring constantly. Remove from heat.
3. Add cereal. Stir until well coated.
4. Coat a 9x13-inch baking pan with butter to prevent the cookies from sticking.
5. Using buttered spatula or waxed paper, press mixture evenly and firmly in buttered 9x13-inch pan.
6. Cut into 2-inch squares when cool.

WEEK 34
DAY 1

I CAN SERVE JESUS AT CHURCH

> *A spiritual gift is given to each of us so we can help each other.*
>
> 1 Corinthians 12:7

Read This!

Pastor Jason was an amazing speaker. It seemed like he didn't even get nervous! He just got up there and made the Bible come alive.

Kristina loved having groups of friends and strangers over to her house after church. She loved baking cookies, making meals, and getting to know new people.

Allie was always encouraging people in her children's church class. Even when she wasn't having a good day, she always had something good to say to others.

Tyler didn't like being in the spotlight. What he did like was helping stack chairs, put out bulletins, and pour up juice for the snack!

God gave each of these people a unique gift. He gave those gifts so they could serve each other and help grow his church! As they served others, they were serving him and showing his love.

Just like God gave Pastor Jason, Kristina, Allie, and Tyler gifts, he's given you gifts, too! How can you use your gift to serve God?

Fear Buster

Sometimes, we feel that we can't do anything for God! We may feel like we're too shy, too young, or not good enough. Thankfully, we don't have to believe that! The Bible tells us God has given each of us gifts to use for him, no matter how we feel.

I CAN SERVE JESUS AT CHURCH

WEEK 34
DAY 2

Try This!

Read this list of gifts commonly talked about in the Bible, and their descriptions. Circle the ones you think are most like you. If one reminds you of someone else, put their name under it!

WISDOM: *The ability to give people good advice that agrees with the Bible.*

FAITH: *The ability to trust God and to help others trust him, too!*

TEACHING: *Helping others understand God's word by teaching it to them.*

SERVING: *Helping out behind the scenes by cleaning, setting up, or doing other hard work.*

GIVING: *Using your money, time, or talents to help others and the church*

LEADERSHIP: *Being able to lead a group of people and help them do a task.*

HOSPITALITY: *Welcoming new people into church, your group, or your home.*

WEEK 34
DAY 3

I CAN SERVE JESUS AT CHURCH

Try This!

What are some ways that you can serve? Use this page to brainstorm some ideas! You can write, draw, or use whatever method works best for you to find a way to serve others.

I CAN SERVE JESUS AT CHURCH

WEEK 34
DAY 4

God is not unjust. He will not forget how hard you have worked for him and how you have shown your love to him by caring for other believers.

Hebrews 6:10

Read This!

Did you know that serving others has a bigger purpose?

When we serve others, we make them feel special and important.

Sometimes, by serving others, we meet a need that they have. If they're hungry and we cook them a meal, we are helping. If they're sad and we encourage them, we're helping!

While those things are good, there is something even better that happens when we serve people. The Bible tells us that when we serve others, we are actually serving God and showing his love.

God created each and every person, so when we serve them, we are showing him how important his creation is. We are showing him how much we love him!

Church is a great opportunity to serve other people. By using our gifts and serving, we are showing them they matter to God and showing God that he matters to us!

Prayer Prompt

Ask God to show you at least one new way you can serve others in your church family!

WEEK 34
DAY 5

I CAN SERVE JESUS AT CHURCH

Try This!

Using the letters of the word SERVANT, write one way you can serve people in your life.

S ______________________________

E ______________________________

R ______________________________

V ______________________________

A ______________________________

N ______________________________

T ______________________________

I CAN SERVE JESUS AT CHURCH

WEEK 34
DAY 6

Try This!

Do you know somebody who serves in your church? See if you can sit down with them to learn more about serving. Here are some things you can ask them:

Name: ______________________________

Age: ______________________________

Job: ______________________________

What do you do to serve in church?

____

____

How does serving make you feel?

____

____

____

Why do you serve others?

____

____

What does serving teach you about God?

____

____

____

WEEK 35
DAY 1

I CAN LEARN ABOUT JESUS AT CHURCH

> *Let the message about Christ, in all its richness, fill your lives. Teach and counsel each other with all the wisdom he gives.*
>
> Colossians 3:16

Read This!

Alecia slouched on the couch and groaned. Her older sister, Melissa, looked up from the book she was reading.

"What's up with you?" she asked.

Alecia sat up. "I'm trying to memorize some verses for Sunday school, but its so hard to read the Bible."

"What do you mean?"

Alecia sighed. "At church, the Bible sounds exciting. We sing songs with the verses in them. We read the verses in groups, and sometimes Miss Elise does funny voices for the characters. Last week, we watched a cool video about spreading the gospel and then talked about applying it to our own lives. But when I sit down with the Bible, I get confused."

Melissa put down her book and faced Alecia. "All those things that you like about church are different ways of connecting with the Bible. If you're intimidated by what you have to memorize, why don't you draw it out? You're always doodling over everything anyway."

Melissa continued. "Make the words stand out to you by putting them in a song or write them in a cool font. If you don't understand the verse, you could always try reading a different translation, too!"

Fear Buster

When you don't know what to do or how to make a decision, God can guide you! He can help you by teaching you through your church family.

I CAN LEARN ABOUT JESUS AT CHURCH

WEEK 35
DAY 2

Try This!

In each of these squares, draw a picture of one of your favorite Bible stories! Practice explaining the story to someone else, teaching them like you're taught at church!

WEEK 35 DAY 3

I CAN LEARN ABOUT JESUS AT CHURCH

Try This!

The Bible calls God's Word a lamp to our feet and light to our path! Tonight when it gets dark, find a flashlight or use the light on your phone. Use it to read a few verses in your Bible. Thank God for the light his Word gives!

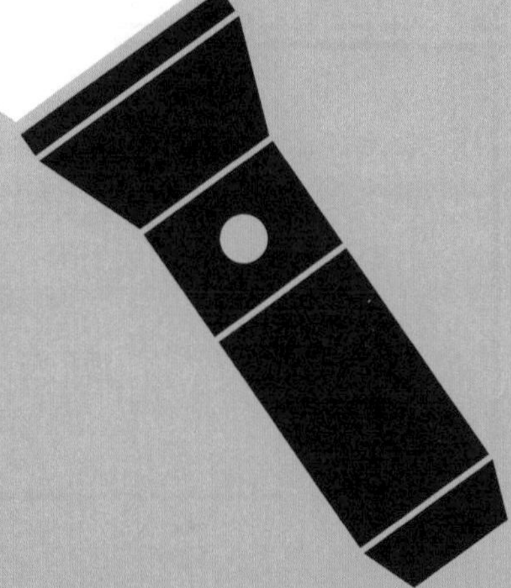

I CAN LEARN ABOUT JESUS AT CHURCH

WEEK 35

DAY 4

Preach the word of God. Be prepared, whether the time is favorable or not. Patiently correct, rebuke, and encourage your people with good teaching.

2 Timothy 4:2

Read This!

Pastors have a special job.

Paul knew that, and that is why he wrote a special letter in the Bible to Timothy, one of the first pastors after Jesus went back to Heaven.

Timothy had a big task in front of him. He needed to tell others about Jesus and help them understand the Bible.

Pastors today still have the same job!

God uses pastors to help others learn about Jesus. They do this through teaching and preaching, when they stand in front of a group or church and help them understand the Bible. This isn't an easy job, but it's an important one!

God uses pastors to help all of us understand more about the Bible. When they are speaking, we can trust that they are working hard to understand God's Word and explain to us what they are learning.

We can thank God for our pastors and pray that he will help them teach his word!

Prayer Prompt

Take some time to pray for your pastors today. Ask God to help them teach you and others the Bible.

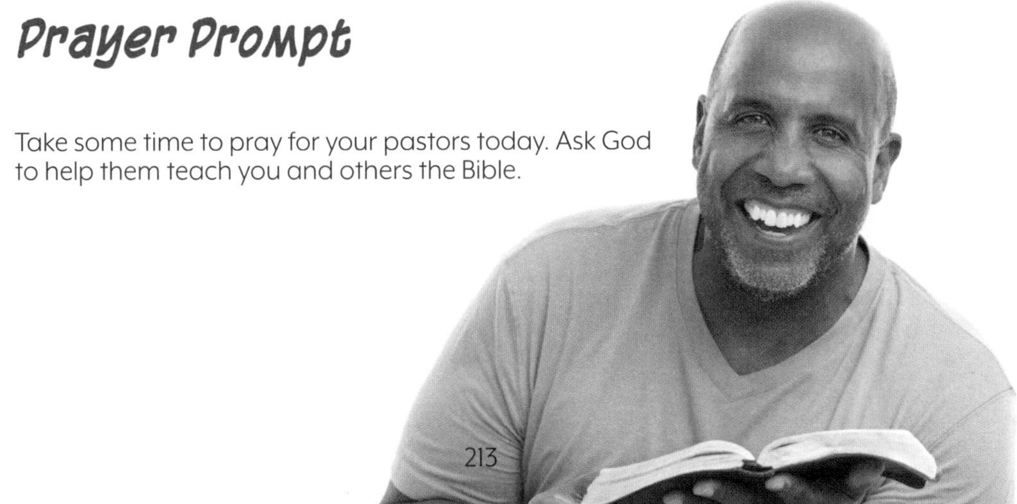

WEEK 35
DAY 5

I CAN LEARN ABOUT JESUS AT CHURCH

Try This!

Take this sheet to church on Sunday, and take some notes on your pastor's sermon!

Sermon Title: ______________________________

Person Preaching: ______________________________

Verses from the Bible: ______________________________

What is an important point from the sermon? ______________________________

____

What are some words I don't understand? ______________________________

____

What is a story they told? ______________________________

____

How can I live this out? ______________________________

____

Draw a picture from the sermon.

I CAN LEARN ABOUT JESUS AT CHURCH

WEEK 35
DAY 6

Try This!

Pastors are very important to the church! On this hand, write five things you are thankful for about your pastor. When you see them, give them a high-five and say thanks for all they do!

WEEK 36 DAY 1

GOD WANTS ME TO WORSHIP HIM

> Great is the LORD! He is most worthy of praise! No one can measure his greatness.
>
> Psalm 145:3

Read This!

Who is the greatest hero you can imagine?

Is it a superhero that you watch on TV or a movie—maybe Batman, Spiderman, or characters from the movies?

Maybe it's a sports star or famous musician, the lead singer of your favorite band or the best player on your hockey team!

Or maybe it's someone in history who's done something great. They invented something cool, fought for human rights, or stood up for what they believed in.

Whoever your hero is, how would you respond if they walked into the room right now? I bet you'd be excited!

You'd probably cheer, yell, give them a hug or high-five, or maybe you'd get really shy and not know what to say. Either way, you would want to show them how amazing they were by your actions.

Our God is the greatest hero we could ever imagine. He is more amazing than any superhero—real or fictional! When we are in his presence, we should show him how great he is by the way we act.

The way we do that is called worship. Worship is when our actions show God how amazing he is! There are lots of ways to worship, but they all come down to one thing— showing God just how super incredible he is!

Fear Buster

Sometimes, when I think of how amazing God is, it makes me nervous! Thankfully, I don't have to be afraid of God. The Bible tells us we can come into his presence boldly and bravely when we worship him!

GOD WANTS ME TO WORSHIP HIM

WEEK 36
DAY 2

Try This!

What are some ways you can worship? Worship doesn't have to involve singing. You can worship God by doing your chores with a cheerful spirit. Set a timer for three minutes and write down as many ways as you can think of that you can worship God! When you've done your list, share it with someone else (or maybe get them to make a list, too!). Brainstorm ways you can worship God.

WEEK 36
DAY 3

GOD WANTS ME TO WORSHIP HIM

Try This!

We worship God because he's amazing and beautiful! One of the ways some churches show God's beauty is by creating stained glass windows with amazing pictures of Bible stories. Create your own stained-glass window in this space to show how amazing God is.

GOD WANTS ME TO WORSHIP HIM

WEEK 36
DAY 4

The time is coming—indeed it's here now—when true worshipers will worship the Father in spirit and in truth. The Father is looking for those who will worship him that way.

John 4:23

Read This!

Abigail had been coming to this same well for years. Today, it felt different. Each day as she walked to the well, she said a prayer. She asked God to make himself real to her. She had made a lot of mistakes in her life, but she wanted to know God. She wanted to give him her life, even if it wasn't easy.

When she arrived at the well, she drew her water like she always did. Then a strange man approached her asking for water. She knew something was different about him.

As he started talking to her, she realized that he had been sent from God! He was the Messiah. When he talked to her about worship, it all made sense. God didn't want some fancy person who was perfect. He just wanted her to worship him.

She had to worship him with her heart and her soul. When she worshiped, it made God happy. It pleased him.

This was the answer Abigail had been looking for. From now on, she would focus on worshiping God. Even if other people didn't understand, she knew he would. Her worship would make God happy, so she would do it.

Prayer Prompt

Thank God that no matter who you are, you can worship him! Spend a few minutes telling him how great he is.

WEEK 36
DAY 5

GOD WANTS ME TO WORSHIP HIM

Try This!

The story of the woman at the well is found in John 4. We don't know the woman's name, but for now let's pretend it's Abigail. Write a letter from Abigail to the people in her town. She wants to share about what Jesus told her, especially about worship!

GOD WANTS ME TO WORSHIP HIM

WEEK 36
DAY 6

Try This!

Amidst all these letters, see how many words you can find about worship! Circle them and then write the words you find on the lines below.

G	O	D	G	E	W	Y	O	G	E	B	X	T	M	E	A	P
F	M	D	O	X	Z	L	M	L	Y	T	S	Z	A	T	O	C
P	U	S	L	D	F	T	J	O	I	A	B	G	G	Q	W	U
R	H	H	H	H	V	K	H	R	D	R	R	G	N	U	Q	C
A	H	P	W	O	D	C	O	I	K	J	F	V	I	U	S	F
Y	N	R	L	O	U	W	N	F	K	F	Y	S	F	C	I	B
B	H	A	O	R	R	T	O	Y	Z	Q	T	D	Y	Q	N	P
D	S	I	H	H	B	S	R	Q	G	U	G	H	X	V	G	L
P	V	S	P	K	O	P	H	P	D	A	N	C	E	W	O	A
O	C	E	W	G	U	L	M	I	B	V	D	J	I	P	B	Y
N	R	T	W	Q	F	E	Y	J	P	M	P	S	W	C	T	P
W	X	L	I	N	S	T	R	U	M	E	N	T	X	U	O	X

Answers on Page 318

WEEK 37
DAY 1

PRAISE JESUS WITH MUSIC AND SINGING

> *His brother's name was Jubal, the first of all who play the harp and flute.*
>
> Genesis 4:21

Read This!

Everyone has their favorite types of music.

Whether it's the beats of hip-hop, the guitars in country, or the loud drums in rock music, there is something about music that connects with us!

Did you know music was God's idea?

In the very first book of the Bible, we see a man named Jubal. He lived at the very beginning of time and was the first person to play music. He played an instrument called a lyre, which had strings like a harp! From then on, people played music to show God how much they loved him!

From drums to cymbals to harps, people used music to worship God! The Bible is full of stories of the music people used and the songs they sang to God. We can still use music to worship God—whether playing an instrument or singing a song, music is an important way to show God how amazing we think he is!

Fear Buster

Did you know that since the Bible times, people have been using music when they were afraid? Singing to God and focusing on him can help us when we're scared. The next time you're feeling afraid, try it!

PRAISE JESUS WITH MUSIC AND SINGING

WEEK 37
DAY 2

Try This!

Have you ever made your own musical instrument? Follow these instructions to make your own tissue box guitar! Once you're done, turn on your favorite worship song and try to play along!

Materials

- Empty tissue box or shoebox
- Scissors
- 4-6 rubber bands

Directions

1. If using a shoebox, cut a small hole in the lid the size of your fist, then stick the lid onto the box. Skip this step if you're using a tissue box—it should already have a hole.
2. Stretch the rubber bands over the box! The rubber bands should go over the hole (this is where the sound will come from).
3. Decorate your box however you'd like. You can even stick a paper towel roll to the top to hold onto!

PRAISE JESUS WITH MUSIC AND SINGING

Try This!

Unscramble the names of these instruments! Use the pictures below if you get stuck. Remember, we can use any of them to praise God!

ARUTIG ____________________

MDURS ____________________

OIPAN ____________________

YMSABLC ____________________

GROAN ____________________

Answers on Page 319

PRAISE JESUS WITH MUSIC AND SINGING

WEEK 37
DAY 4

Then I will praise God's name with singing, and I will honor him with thanksgiving. For this will please the Lord.

Psalm 69:30-31

Read This!

Trey stood in church on Sunday morning with the rest of his church family. The pastor opened the service in prayer and then the music started!

Everyone began to sing. Some were clapping, and some stood with their hands by their sides. A few people had their hands raised high, while others had their eyes closed, just listening. A couple of his mom's friends were dancing to the beat, while most people just stood still.

Trey liked music and singing, but this seemed different than other music. People weren't just singing along or listening like they were at a concert. They were singing to someone.

All of a sudden, Trey realized who they were singing to! It was Jesus! The dancing, the clapping, even the quiet listening, was a way of using music to talk to God! His church was using music to show God how important he was and how much they loved him.

Trey loved music, and he loved God even more! He could use music to worship God, too. He put his hands together and started to clap as the next song started. What a cool way to give thanks to his incredible God!

Prayer Prompt

Instead of praying, put on a worship song and sing it to God!

PRAISE JESUS WITH MUSIC AND SINGING

Try This!

Write the words to your favorite worship song or hymn below. Read them over, and then write about what those words mean to you.

PRAISE JESUS WITH MUSIC AND SINGING

WEEK 37
DAY 6

Try This!

What songs do you love that worship Jesus? Write down your five favorite songs about Jesus! If you're feeling brave, share them with a friend so they can hear about how amazing Jesus is!

WEEK 38
DAY 1

I CAN PRAISE JESUS BY GIVING

> They must not appear before the LORD without a gift for him. All must give as they are able, according to the blessings given to them by the LORD your God.
>
> Deuteronomy 16:16-17

Read This!

"Do you think Kayla would like princess things or beach things?" Mom asked Lacey. Lacey looked around at the toys in the aisle and thought about her best friend.

"We don't really play princess that much anymore," Lacey thought aloud. "I just want to get her the best birthday gift ever! She's my favorite person and I want her to be excited by what I pick."

Mom started moving to the next aisle and Lacey followed close behind. "Also, I've been saving my allowance for two months and I really want to make this gift worth it."

Mom and Lacey browsed through aisles of movies, board games, video games, building sets, and awesome outdoor toys. Then, they found a beach bag that would match Kayla's surf board.

"It's perfect!" Lacey cheered and quickly counted her money. She didn't have that much, but it was enough for the bag and a pair of sparkly sunglasses. She hoped Kayla would know she gave her the best gift she could afford, even if it wasn't the snazziest gift in the store.

Just like Lacey gave her friend the best gift she could, God wants our best gifts, too! God isn't concerned with the amount of time or money we give him. All he wants is our very best. Giving God our best is one way we show him how super incredible he is!

Fear Buster

We never have to worry if God will look at us differently because we can't give as much money or time as someone else. All he asks for is our best!

I CAN PRAISE JESUS BY GIVING

WEEK 38
DAY 2

Try This!

Write labels for each of these pictures. What are these people giving to God?

I CAN PRAISE JESUS BY GIVING

Try This!

What is the BEST thing you can give God? In each of these gift boxes, draw a picture or write a sentence of what you can give.

I CAN PRAISE JESUS BY GIVING

WEEK 38
DAY 4

God loves a person who gives cheerfully.
2 Corinthians 9:7

Read This!

William was so excited! He had counted his birthday money over and over. For the first time ever, he had one hundred dollars of his own. He couldn't stop imagining all the things he could buy.

As William was making a list of the things he would buy, he remembered the special missions project they were doing at church. His pastor had announced that they were collecting money to send to a missionary in Guatemala! The money would help buy school supplies for kids who couldn't afford any.

William had an idea! Instead of spending all his birthday money on himself, he would give half of it to that missions project. He had lots of stuff already. Giving that money to missions would make God happy, and it would make those kids happy.

William didn't give because he had to. He gave because he wanted to. It made him happy to share what he had with others. William did a super incredible thing for our super incredible God!

Prayer Prompt

Ask God what you can give to show him your love!

WEEK 38
DAY 5

I CAN PRAISE JESUS BY GIVING

Try This!

The Bible tells us that God loves it when we give to him! What do you think God would say to you when you give to him? Write it down! Include some fun art with what you write!

I CAN PRAISE JESUS BY GIVING

WEEK 38
DAY 6

Try This!

One of the things we can give to God is money! If you had a million dollars, what would you do with it? What kinds of things would you give to? Write it down here! Even though you don't have a million dollars, think of some ways you can give to God!

WEEK 39
DAY 1

I CAN PRAISE JESUS BY LIVING FOR HIM

> *Let everything that breathes sing praises to the LORD!*
> Psalm 150:6

Read This!

How many times do you think worship is mentioned in the Bible? Have any guesses?

Would you believe that it is mentioned over eight thousand times? That is a lot! This tells us that worship isn't just something we should do sometimes, or even on Sundays. Worship is important in the Bible, which means it's important to God! That means it should be important to us.

Our God is so amazing that he deserves to be worshiped every single day! We don't just worship when we feel like it, or even just when we are at church. We worship God every day! We can do that through our singing, through our giving, and through the way we live!

Your challenge is simple: How can you worship God today? How can you show him that you love him?

Fear Buster

Did you know that in the Bible, when people were scared, they worshiped God? It helped them focus on God and not be afraid! Today, if you feel scared, worship God!

I CAN PRAISE JESUS BY LIVING FOR HIM

WEEK 39
DAY 2

Try This!

The book of Psalms is full of songs that worship God! Write your own psalm to God, telling him how amazing he is! Choose a few psalms from the Bible to read for inspiration before you begin.

WEEK 39
DAY 3

I CAN PRAISE JESUS BY LIVING FOR HIM

Try This!

What does your schedule look like every day? Write down what your average day looks like (you can include pictures if you want!) After you've written it down, try to come up with some ways you can worship God during your day. Include them in your schedule!

I CAN PRAISE JESUS BY LIVING FOR HIM

WEEK 39
DAY 4

Give your bodies to God because of all he has done for you. Let them be a living and holy sacrifice—the kind he will find acceptable. This is truly the way to worship him.

Romans 12:1

Read This!

Before Sienna got out of bed in the morning, she whispered a quick prayer: "Jesus, help me live my life for you today!"

When Levi arrived at school, he listened to his teacher even when he didn't want to. He was trying to honor his leaders because that's what God asked him to do.

During her lunch break, Alexandria opened her Bible and started to read. She wouldn't have much free time after school today, but she wanted to take a few minutes to spend with Jesus while she could!

Bennett practiced his song for guitar lessons really hard after school. He knew that if he kept practicing and doing his best, he'd be able to play in church someday and worship Jesus with the band! For now, he'd worship Jesus while he played in his room.

Each of these kids knew that worshiping Jesus needed to be a part of their everyday lives. They did that through their words, their actions, and the way they lived their lives. Everyday life is their worship, and it can be yours, too!

Prayer Prompt

Ask God to help you live every day as worship to him.

WEEK 39
DAY 5

I CAN PRAISE JESUS BY LIVING FOR HIM

Try This!

In the word search, find the words below from Romans 12:1. Write the whole verse on the lines below when you're done.

J	Q	E	W	T	C	R	F	F	L	D	T	Q	Z	L	V	T	B
R	D	T	N	O	H	O	A	R	G	A	L	D	J	M	J	Z	E
E	S	X	Z	Y	R	P	T	W	F	C	V	M	L	W	B	T	J
G	T	A	D	L	H	S	S	Z	V	C	G	S	M	P	Q	X	N
Y	N	C	C	P	I	V	H	A	P	E	F	H	R	T	R	H	Q
Y	B	J	U	R	L	V	E	I	V	P	G	H	D	K	V	O	H
A	Z	O	H	B	I	B	I	M	P	T	T	E	R	O	V	L	Q
P	X	G	D	M	L	F	Q	N	E	A	E	R	E	Y	T	Y	Z
Y	G	E	I	I	R	T	I	V	G	B	G	A	U	G	V	B	N
D	O	V	E	V	E	F	H	C	L	L	H	W	L	L	G	E	J
O	D	W	V	R	E	S	B	F	E	E	A	A	A	O	Y	V	R
W	Y	S	M	A	K	V	L	A	N	D	I	P	C	K	N	L	R

Give	Living	Acceptable
Bodies	Sacrifice	Truly
God	Holy	Worship

Answers on Page 319

I CAN PRAISE JESUS BY LIVING FOR HIM

WEEK 39
DAY 6

Try This!

Draw six scenes with a picture of you doing something to worship Jesus!

WEEK 40 DAY 1

GOD IS WITH ME WHEN HARD TIMES COME

Be sure of this: I am with you always, even to the end of the age.
Matthew 28:20

Read This!

Raine's dad lost his job last week. Even though her parents were trying to act tough, she could tell they were scared. Raine had a younger brother and sister, and she knew that her parents needed money to keep everything going.

She had heard some friends at school talk about how their mom or dad had to move away when they had lost their job. Some of her friends had even had to move to a new state or country in the middle of the school year. That was a scary thought. Raine couldn't imagine leaving her house, her friends, or her church.

Raine was trying really hard to be brave, but she'd never faced something like this before! She was just plain scared.

That week at her kids' small group, she shared how she was feeling. Raine told the group that she was nervous of where her family might end up or what would happen. While Raine's leader couldn't guarantee what would happen, she could promise one thing. No matter what happened to Raine and her family, Jesus would be with her! He promised it in the Bible, and Raine could count on that promise.

Even though Raine was still nervous, she knew she could trust Jesus. He would be with her, no matter what!

Fear Buster

All of us face scary situations in our lives where we don't know what will happen! Even when we don't know how things will turn out, we can trust that Jesus will be with us.

GOD IS WITH ME WHEN HARD TIMES COME

WEEK 40
DAY 2

Try This!

Jesus promised his disciples, and he promises us, that he will be with us always! On this time line, write some of the major things that have happened in your life. For example, being born, getting a brother or sister, starting school, or moving to a town. As you write each one, remember that God has been with you through them all.

Born

Today

GOD IS WITH ME WHEN HARD TIMES COME

Try This!

In our devotional, Raine was pretty nervous about her parents losing their jobs and her family having to move. If you could write a letter to Raine to encourage her, what would you say?

GOD IS WITH ME WHEN HARD TIMES COME

WEEK 40
DAY 4

If we are thrown into the blazing furnace, the God whom we serve is able to save us. He will rescue us.

Daniel 3:17

Read This!

Shadrach, Meshach, and Abednego were, for the most part, regular teenagers.

They were good friends, who loved to spend time together. They loved God and worshiped him.

One thing made these three boys different—they had been taken away from their home country and were living in a strange land under a harsh king! That king didn't worship their God, and he didn't want anyone else worshiping him, either.

The king decided that he would build a giant statue of himself, and every person who lived in his country would have to bow down and worship it! Anyone who didn't would be thrown into a giant furnace.

Doesn't that sound terrifying? I bet Shadrach, Meshach, and Abednego were scared! They didn't let their fear stop them from trusting God, though. Even though they were facing a really scary time, they knew God was on their side. They refused to worship the statue!

The king threw the three boys into the fire—but they survived! God showed up and kept them safe. Soon, even the king was worshiping their God.

Even though they lived thousands of years ago, we can be like Shadrach, Meshach, and Abednego and trust God no matter what comes our way!

Prayer Prompt

Are you facing a hard time right now? Pray a simple prayer: "God, I trust you!"

GOD IS WITH ME WHEN HARD TIMES COME

Try This!

Read the whole story of Shadrach, Meshach, and Abednego in Daniel 3. Once you've read it, draw a poster that shows them worshiping the true God and tells their story of trusting God.

GOD IS WITH ME WHEN HARD TIMES COME

WEEK 40
DAY 6

Try This!

The story of Shadrach, Meshach, and Abednego reminds us that God is with us in our hard times! Draw the three of them standing in the flames below. Finish this picture of them in the fire by adding God to the picture!

WEEK 41 DAY 1

JESUS CAN HELP ME THROUGH HARD TIMES

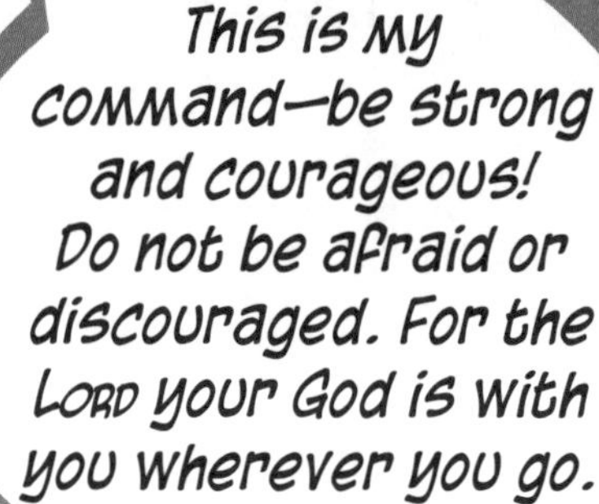

Read This!

"What does *diabetes* mean?" Lakyn asked Doctor Jen, who had just told her the name of her condition.

Doctor Jen smiled. "It just means that your body doesn't break down food the way that it is supposed to."

Lakyn rubbed her sweaty palms on her legs. Doctor Jen quickly added, "But don't worry, lots of people have diabetes. You can live pretty much like other people, there are just certain foods you should stay away from. Also, you'll have to give yourself an insulin shot a few times a day."

Lakyn's eyes began to water. Her mom pulled her close and rubbed her back.

Doctor Jen took Lakyn's hand. "Don't worry, I know it sounds scary, but the insulin will make you feel so much better."

Lakyn just closed her eyes and leaned into her mom. She hated needles. She didn't care if they would make her feel better.

Later that night, Lakyn whispered a prayer in bed.

"Jesus, please make me brave!" As she prayed, she knew that Jesus was with her. Even though the needles still hurt, she knew she could count on God to give her courage and help her be brave.

What is happening in your life that is hard or scary? Just like Jesus gave Lakyn courage, he can give it to you, too!

Fear Buster

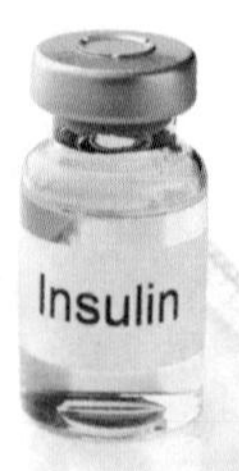

Jesus promises to give us courage when things are scary! No matter what you face, you can ask God to make you brave.

JESUS CAN HELP ME THROUGH HARD TIMES

WEEK 41
DAY 2

Try This!

Do you know the stories of these people in the Bible who were brave? If not, look up the verses next to their name. Write one sentence that describes how they showed courage.

David (1 Samuel 17)

____

____

Esther (Esther 5)

____

____

King Josiah (2 Kings 22)

____

____

Peter (Acts 2)

____

____

Abigail (1 Samuel 25)

____

____

WEEK 41

DAY 3

JESUS CAN HELP ME THROUGH HARD TIMES

Can you make up a rhythm or rhyme to help you remember this verse? Say it or chant it when you're in a scary situation!

This is my command—be strong and courageous! Do not be afraid or discouraged. For the LORD your God is with you wherever you go.

Joshua 1:9

JESUS CAN HELP ME THROUGH HARD TIMES

WEEK 41
DAY 4

I am leaving you with a gift—peace of mind and heart. And the peace I give is a gift the world cannot give. So don't be troubled or afraid.
John 14:27

Read This!

Tyrell had knots in his stomach. His palms felt sweaty, and he wished he could just run away! It was his first day at his new church, and he was so scared.

When his family had moved to their new city a few weeks ago, Tyrell felt excited. His new room was awesome, and there was a cool park just down the street. He didn't feel excited today, though—he felt scared.

Tyrell loved his old church and his pastors there. He knew all the songs that they sang, and he had friends that he sat with each week during the kids' time. He wouldn't know anyone at this new church! He wished he could just stay home.

As he walked through the parking lot with his family, Tyrell remembered the words his old pastor had said when he was getting ready to leave. He'd told Tyrell that Jesus promised to give him peace no matter where he was. All he had to do was ask him!

Well, if there was ever a time Tyrell needed to feel peace, it was now. He said a prayer as he marched across the parking lot.

At first, the prayer didn't really feel like it worked. He still had knots in his stomach, and he still wanted to go home. After a few minutes though, Tyrell felt a strange sense of peace inside. He knew that no matter what happened, Jesus would be close to him. And that was the most important thing of all!

Prayer Prompt

Pray and ask God to give peace to people who are facing scary situations today!

WEEK 41
DAY 5

JESUS CAN HELP ME THROUGH HARD TIMES

Try This!

God's peace is with you! Color in or create cool designs in the words below to help you remember that truth!

GOD'S PEACE IS WITH ME

JESUS CAN HELP ME THROUGH HARD TIMES

WEEK 41
DAY 6

Try This!

Have you ever received a secret message from a friend? Receiving a secret message can make us feel so special!

Create your own special code using pictures for this verse from John. Use symbols that would make sense to someone else. Then, let them try to figure it out!

I am leaving you with a gift—peace of mind and heart. And the peace I give is a gift the world cannot give. So don't be troubled or afraid.

John 14:27

WEEK 42
DAY 1

I CAN BRING MY QUESTIONS TO JESUS

> If you need wisdom, ask our generous God, and he will give it to you. He will not rebuke you for asking.
>
> James 1:9

Read This!

Lia had a big decision to make! Her parents had decided to separate, and her mom was moving to a brand new city a couple of hours away.

She knew she would still get to see both her mom and dad, but she had to decide who she wanted to stay with for most of the time. Wherever she chose, she would be going to school there.

This was a really hard and really confusing decision! She loved both her mom and dad so much, and she didn't want to have to choose. She loved her house, her school, and her friends, but she also loved her mom. She couldn't imagine being far away from her!

Lia really didn't know what to do. So she did the only thing she knew how to—she prayed and asked God to help her. "Lord, I'm so confused and upset. I don't know how to make this decision. Please give me peace. Remind me that you are always with me."

Even though her situation wasn't any different when she finished praying, she felt better knowing God was with her and understood what she was facing.

Fear Buster

Even as kids, we can face really tough decisions that cause us to ask a lot of questions! When we don't know what to do, we can go to Jesus. He will help us and give us his presence.

I CAN BRING MY QUESTIONS TO JESUS

WEEK 42
DAY 2

Try This!

God is big enough to handle any of our questions! In fact, he's the only one wise enough to give us answers. Inside these giant question marks, make a list of questions you'd like to ask God. Then, next time you pray, actually ask him those questions!

WEEK 42
DAY 3

I CAN BRING MY QUESTIONS TO JESUS

Try This!

God can give wisdom in each of these situations. Next to each of these pictures, write one sentence of wisdom that you think God would give!

I CAN BRING MY QUESTIONS TO JESUS

WEEK 42
DAY 4

> *How long, O Lord, must I call for help? But you do not listen!*
>
> Habakkuk 1:2

Read This!

Marcus was so mad! He had worked hard all year to become the best hockey player he could be.

He never missed a practice, he worked hard in every game, and he even saved up his birthday money to buy new equipment. He had missed all kinds of fun stuff—birthday parties and after school hangouts—to go to hockey school and special training.

So, he couldn't believe it when his coach told him that he hadn't made the All-Star team! He had worked so hard! He couldn't believe this was happening to him.

Life was so unfair. Other kids who had made the team didn't work as hard as he did, and one of them hadn't even scored a goal all season.

Marcus had never felt this way before. He was super angry! He felt like crying and yelling all at once. He didn't know what to do to calm down, so he did the only thing he could think of. He prayed.

He told God exactly how he was feeling. He talked to God about how angry he was and how disappointed he felt. He even said he might never play hockey again!

Even though Marcus was really angry, he knew God could handle it! God cared about him and wanted to know exactly how he was feeling.

Prayer Prompt

How was your day today? Talk to God about it. Telling him all about it and how it made you feel! There's nothing that we need to hide from him.

I CAN BRING MY QUESTIONS TO JESUS

Try This!

Sometimes, it can be hard to describe exactly how we're feeling. Choose words from the word bank below and draw lines to the appropriate faces. No matter how you feel, you can talk to God about it!

Angry

Embarrassed

Disappointed

Sad

Surprised

Glad

Devastated

Silly

Confused

Answers on Page 318

I CAN BRING MY QUESTIONS TO JESUS

WEEK 42
DAY 6

Try This!

When we feel angry, we need to get it out in a healthy way before we explode! Here are some ways we can get out your anger. With permission from a grown-up, try one today, and then try some again when you're actually feeling angry:

- Do jumping jacks
- Rip a piece of paper
- Pop bubble wrap
- Squish or modeling clay
- Squeeze a stress ball
- Take deep breaths
- Jump on a trampoline

WEEK 43
DAY 1

JESUS IS BIG ENOUGH TO HANDLE MY DOUBTS

Show mercy to those whose faith is wavering.

Jude 1:22

Read This!

Even though Chrissy loved Jesus, there were some days when she had a lot of questions

Sometimes, it was hard to trust in a God she couldn't see. When so many of her friends didn't believe in Jesus, sometimes it felt like it would be easier just to quit!

She loved the Bible and learning from it, but some things were hard to understand. Did those things really happen? What did those confusing stories in the Old Testament even mean?

While Chrissy had all kinds of questions, she was scared to ask anyone about them! She didn't want them to think she was a bad Christian or that she didn't love Jesus. She really did, but she felt confused about some things.

One day, Chrissy told her older sister about how she was feeling. She told her that she had some hard questions about following Jesus, and sometimes, she didn't feel like believing in him. Chrissy thought her sister would get upset or tell her she was a bad Christian, but instead, she reached over and gave her a huge hug!

Her sister told her that asking questions and having doubts was totally normal. The important thing was bringing them to the right person, and that person was Jesus! He loved Chrissy enough to hear all of her questions and doubts. He would be with her and help her as she worked through this. He is such a super incredible God!

Fear Buster

It can feel scary when we have questions about God. We might wonder if it makes us a bad Christian. Thankfully, God loves us enough to handle all of our questions. Instead of being scared, ask your questions to Jesus!

JESUS IS BIG ENOUGH TO HANDLE MY DOUBTS

WEEK 43
DAY 2

Try This!

Sometimes, we doubt God because we can't see him or what he's doing in our lives! Thankfully, even when we can't see him, we can know he's working. Try out this cool invisible ink activity to remind yourself that even when we can't see what God is doing, he's still at work.

Materials

- 1 lemon, cut in half
- water
- spoon
- small bowl
- cotton swab
- white paper
- lamp

Directions

1. Squeeze both halves of your lemon into the bowl.
2. Add 2 or 3 drops of water to the lemon juice, and mix with a spoon.
3. Dip the cotton swab into the mixture.
4. Write your message on the paper.
5. Hold your paper up to the light. After a little bit your message will show up on the paper!

JESUS IS BIG ENOUGH TO HANDLE MY DOUBTS

Try This!

One of the ways that we can deal with doubt is by talking to someone else who has doubted! Write down three questions who follows Jesus! Write down their answers on this page.

1. ______________________________

____

____

2. ______________________________

____

____

3. ______________________________

____

____

JESUS IS BIG ENOUGH TO HANDLE MY DOUBTS

WEEK 43
DAY 4

[Jesus] said to Thomas . . . "Don't be faithless any longer. Believe!"

John 20:27

Read This!

Thomas couldn't believe what his friends were telling him!

They claimed that Jesus—the one they had seen killed a few days before —was alive again. More than that, they said he had showed up when they were meeting together.

Even though Thomas wanted to believe them, it sounded too good to be true. Jesus couldn't really be alive, could he? He had seen what happened on the cross. How could this be possible?

Thomas finally told his friends, "Unless I see him and touch him, I won't believe you!"

A week later, Thomas could hardly believe it when Jesus showed up at a meeting with his friends! The doors were all locked, but Jesus was somehow there!

Jesus stood in the middle of them and reached out to Thomas! "Thomas, you can touch me! You can see me! Stop doubting—I'm alive!"

Thomas was overwhelmed. Jesus was really alive! More than that, Jesus loved him enough to show up and put his doubts to rest. He knew that he could always trust Jesus.

Prayer Prompt

Thank God that no matter what questions and doubts you have, he loves you and shows up!

JESUS IS BIG ENOUGH TO HANDLE MY DOUBTS

Try This!

Draw what you think the disciples' faces looked like when Jesus showed up! Make sure you choose one to be Thomas, and especially focus on his face! How would he feel when Jesus showed up?

JESUS IS BIG ENOUGH TO HANDLE MY DOUBTS

WEEK 43
DAY 6

Try This!

Thomas said in order to believe in Jesus, he needed to touch the scars on his hands! We can put our doubts in Jesus' hands. On this picture of Jesus' hand, trace your own hand inside. Write a statement above the hands saying you will give your doubts to Jesus.

I CAN SHARE JESUS WHEN I AM BAPTIZED

WEEK 44
DAY 1

Read This!

When they confessed their sins, he baptized them in the Jordan River.
Matthew 3:6

John the Baptist stood on the shores of the Jordan River. People must have wondered what he was doing. He didn't cut his hair, and he wore clothes made out of camel hair. He even ate bugs!

But John had a purpose straight from God. He called people to confess their sins, turn from their old ways, and be baptized. As they went under the water, it was a sign that they were sorry, and their sins were gone away. Hundreds of people were baptized by John.

After Jesus came, his followers continued to baptize people who walked away from their sins. The churches in the New Testament and all throughout history have baptized people to show that their sins are taken away by Jesus.

Baptism is a sign that Jesus has changed our lives. Our sins are gone, and we belong to Jesus.

What a great way to show people how our super incredible God can change our lives!

Fear Buster

Being baptized can be a scary thing. It happens in front of people, and you have to go into water! Thankfully, God promises to be with us at all times, including when we are baptized!

I CAN SHARE JESUS WHEN I AM BAPTIZED

WEEK 44
DAY 2

Try This!

Read the story of John the Baptist in Matthew 3. Then, draw a picture and make a caption for the story. If people had been taking pictures and posting them online, what would they have said? What would it have looked like?

WEEK 44
DAY 3

I CAN SHARE JESUS WHEN I AM BAPTIZED

Try This!

Being baptized is a sign that our sins are taken away! In this picture of a river, write all the sins that Jesus can take away. Think of as many as you possibly can. There is no sin too great that Jesus can't take it away!

I CAN SHARE JESUS WHEN I AM BAPTIZED

WEEK 44
DAY 4

Have you forgotten that when we were joined with Christ Jesus in baptism, we joined him in his death?

Romans 6:3

Read This!

Talia had been a Christian for two years. She had decided to follow Jesus at Vacation Bible School. Since then, she had been growing in her relationship with God!

She knew that Jesus loved her more than she could even imagine, and she wanted to do everything she could to love him back!

She started going to church with her friends so that she could learn more about Jesus. Each night before she went to sleep, she read something out of the Bible she had gotten from her small group leader.

Even though her mom and dad weren't Christians, they told her that she was different since she'd started following Jesus! She seemed like she was happier, she cared more about others, and she wanted to do everything she could to please God.

When Talia heard they were having a water baptism service at church, she wanted to be a part of it! Her small group leader explained that being baptized was an important part of following Jesus. It showed the people around her that she had a new life in Jesus. It was an outward sign of the inward change she had experienced.

When the Sunday came for Talia to be baptized, her parents came to church and sat in the front row. She was so glad she could show them the new life she had in Jesus, and she hoped they would find it, too.

Prayer Prompt

Thank God for the new life you have in Jesus!

I CAN SHARE JESUS WHEN I AM BAPTIZED

WEEK 44
DAY 5

Try This!

Have you ever seen someone get baptized before? If you have, describe what it was like on the lines below! If you haven't seen someone be baptized, use the lines to write down some questions you have about what happens when someone gets baptized.

I CAN SHARE JESUS WHEN I AM BAPTIZED

WEEK 44
DAY 6

Try This!

Complete this crossword puzzle about baptism!

Across

2. Talia got baptized at her _____

5. Baptism shows others that I _____ Jesus

7. The wet stuff!

8. Baptism is a sign that our _____ are taken away

Down

1. The person who baptized Jesus

3. The kind of hair that John's clothes were made of

4. The river where John baptized people

6. Who gives us new life?

9. When we follow Jesus, we have _____ life!

Answers on Page 318

WEEK 45
DAY 1

I AM A WITNESS FOR JESUS

> Thank the Lord! Praise his name! Tell the nations what he has done. Let them know how mighty he is!
> Isaiah 12:4

Read This!

Ivy took a deep breath and started to talk. This was the moment she had been waiting for.

Her big sister, Eliza, was home from college, and she wanted to talk to Ivy. Eliza had heard from their parents that Ivy was going to church, and she wanted to know why.

Honestly, Ivy wasn't really sure what to say. She wished she had paid more attention in church, or learned more Bible verses. But she hadn't! Instead, she just started telling Eliza about what she knew about Jesus and all the amazing things he had done.

She told Eliza about Jesus' love, the fact that he had made the world, and all the miracles he'd done! She told her about how he had died on the cross, but now he was alive again and in Heaven with God.

When Eliza asked her why she went to church, she just told her that she wanted to know more about this amazing God! Ivy couldn't help but get excited when she heard about him.

Even though Eliza didn't say anything about following Jesus, she seemed interested. Ivy knew she would keep telling Eliza about this super incredible God!

Fear Buster

Telling people about Jesus can be scary! When we don't know what to do or say, we can just tell them about how amazing our God is.

Try This!

Create a comic strip of Ivy and Eliza's conversation!
Include speech bubbles and fun drawings.

WEEK 45
DAY 3

I AM A WITNESS FOR JESUS

Try This!

Unscramble the words from Jesus to his disciples right before he went back to Heaven. It's a message for us, too!

___

EH LDOT MHET, "OG

___

ONTI LAL ETH DROLW

___

NAD HRCPAE EHT OODG

___

EWNS OT EEEYNORV."

Mark 16:15

Answers on Page 319

I AM A WITNESS FOR JESUS

WEEK 45
DAY 4

Jesus told him, "I am the way, the truth, and the life. No one can come to the Father except through me."
John 14:6

Read This!

Georgia was excited and nervous, all at the same time.

She had been practicing telling the story of Jesus at children's church for weeks now. Her teacher and the other kids in her class had been helping each other learn how to tell other people about Jesus.

They learned to tell about how we all need Jesus and how because he died, rose again, and was now in Heaven, we could know God and be saved forever!

It was an amazing story, and it was one that had changed Georgia and her family. She couldn't wait to share it with other people! So, when her friend Chelsey asked her about church and why she went, she knew it was the perfect opportunity.

Georgia asked Chelsey if it was okay if she told her a little bit about Jesus. When Chelsey said yes, Georgia started to tell her about the things she'd been learning. She did her best to tell her everything. As they talked, Chelsey asked her some questions. Georgia didn't know all the answers, but she told her she would find out!

At the end of the conversation, Georgia invited Chelsey to come to church with her on Sunday. She said they could talk about this any time she wanted, and that she'd love to help Chelsey learn more about Jesus. Chelsea seemed excited, and so was Georgia. It was a super incredible feeling to tell a friend about Jesus!

Prayer Prompt

Ask God to lead you to someone who needs to hear the good news of Jesus! Ask him to give you courage to tell them when you have the opportunity.

WEEK 45 DAY 5

I AM A WITNESS FOR JESUS

Try This!

Have you ever heard of the Wordless Book? It is a very popular tool that has been used for hundreds of years to share the Gospel with people—especially kids! The Wordless Book has pages of different colored paper. Each colorful page represents a different part of Jesus' story. Below are the colors and what they stand for. Color each block according to the color listed in capital letters! Tomorrow, you'll make your own Wordless Book craft.

GOLD or YELLOW stands for Heaven. Heaven is a wonderful place, and it's God's home! God wants all of us to be in Heaven with him, but there is something that keeps us from being able to go to Heaven with him.
BLACK stands for what keeps us from being with God—sin. Sin is what we do that hurts God and keeps us far away from him. All of us have sinned. We cannot get rid of our sin on our own!
RED stands for Jesus and the way he saved us from our sins! Jesus is God's Son who came to Earth. He died on the cross for us to get rid of all the wrong things we did. He took our place!
WHITE is what happens to our hearts when we accept what Jesus did for us. Because he died on the cross, our hearts can be made clean from all our sin. We can know God. This happens when we accept Jesus into our lives, telling him we've done wrong and that we want him to be in charge!
GREEN reminds us of things that grow, like grass, leaves, and trees! When we accept Jesus as a part of our lives, we can grow in our relationship with him!

I AM A WITNESS FOR JESUS

WEEK 45
DAY 6

Try This!

Create your own version of the Wordless Book using colorful building bricks!

USE THE YELLOW BRICKS TO MAKE A HOUSE. THIS YELLOW HOUSE REPRESENTS HEAVEN.

USE THE BLACK BRICKS TO MAKE A HEART. THIS BLACK HEART REPRESENTS SIN.

USE THE RED BRICKS TO MAKE A CROSS. THIS RED CROSS REPRESENTS THE BLOOD OF JESUS.

USE THE WHITE BRICKS TO MAKE A HEART. THIS WHITE HEART REPRESENTS A CLEAN HEART.

USE THE GREEN BRICKS TO MAKE A TREE. THIS GREEN TREE REPRESENTS GROWTH.

WEEK 46

DAY 1

I CAN SHARE JESUS WITH MY STORY

Instead, you must worship Christ as Lord of your life. And if someone asks about your hope as a believer, always be ready to explain it.

1 Peter 3:15

Read This!

"Lucy, why do you follow Jesus?" asked Lucy's friend, Griffin.

Lucy was surprised when Griffin asked her the question. He never seemed to care when she talked about her church or her kids group, but right now, he seemed really interested.

When she started to tell him about her church, he stopped her. "No, Lucy. I don't want to know about church. I want to know why YOU follow Jesus!"

Lucy paused. She had to be more personal. But how? She realized that this was an opportunity to tell Griffin how Jesus had changed her life.

"Well, my family used to argue all the time." Lucy began, "I was always fighting with my brother and my parents yelled a lot. But since we've gone to church, everything has been much calmer. My parents are happier and I'm more patient with my brother. Even when my dad lost his job last year, we knew that God would take care of us. It was still a scary time, but my family stayed faithful."

At the end of her story, Griffin said "Wow, Lucy! That's really cool. I can see now why you always talk about church and God. He's really amazing. I'd like to know more about him."

Lucy and Griffin decided to meet up the next day after school to play and talk more about God. Lucy was so excited! The story of her super incredible faith had helped show Griffin how amazing Jesus was!

Fear Buster

Sharing the story of Jesus with our friends can be pretty intimidating! Thankfully, we don't need to have our words perfect. All we need to do is ask God to be with us and tell the truth.

I CAN SHARE JESUS WITH MY STORY

WEEK 46
DAY 2

Try This!

Imagine that the story of what Jesus has done in your life was on a newspaper's front page. Write down what you think the reporter would say. Be sure to include a headline and a front page picture with a caption.

Current Press

DAILY NEWS

All news in one newspaper

Issue: 240460

WEEK 46
DAY 3

I CAN SHARE JESUS WITH MY STORY

Try This!

Try to write your story using just five sentences! For a bonus, see if you can start each sentence with the letters of the word STORY.

S ______________________________

T ______________________________

O ______________________________

R ______________________________

Y ______________________________

I CAN SHARE JESUS WITH MY STORY

WEEK 46
DAY 4

The Holy Spirit will teach you at that time what needs to be said.

Luke 12:12

Read This!

Lindsey was so mad at herself! She froze every time she had a chance to tell other people about Jesus.

She couldn't get her words out, she stuttered and stammered, and she ended up just walking away. It was super embarrassing. Plus, she felt like she was letting God down.

Why couldn't she just get it together? It should be easy to share her story! Why was she so scared?

A few days later, Lindsey had a chance to tell one of her friends about Jesus. They were talking about religions and which one they followed. When it was her turn, Lindsey decided to do something different. Before she told her story, she whispered a quick prayer, asking God to help her know what to say.

This time, everything felt different. Even though she still stumbled over some of her words, it was like God was guiding her! She knew exactly what to say. It was amazing!

Maybe you feel like Lindsey, and it's hard to share the story of what Jesus has done for you with others. Ask God to help you. He promises his Holy Spirit will give us the words to say when we need them!

Prayer Prompt

Ask the Holy Spirit to give you the words to say the next time you have the chance to share the story of what Jesus has done in your life!

I CAN SHARE JESUS WITH MY STORY

Try This!

Imagine that your life was a chapter book. What would the different chapters be called. Create a table of contents for the chapters of your life. God is a part of every chapter in your story!

I CAN SHARE JESUS WITH MY STORY

WEEK 46
DAY 6

Try This!

Sometimes worship songs can help us tell others what Jesus did for us! If you had to make a playlist with FIVE songs that would tell the story of what Jesus did for you, what would they be?

1. ______________________________

2. ______________________________

3. ______________________________

4. ______________________________

5. ______________________________

WEEK 47
DAY 1

I AM WILLING TO GO WHERE JESUS SENDS ME

> [Isaiah] said, "Here I am. Send me."
>
> Isaiah 6:8

Read This!

God's people needed someone to preach his message to them! He needed them to know that God wanted them to change their ways. He needed someone to tell them that God had a plan for them and that he wanted to save them.

That someone was Isaiah. He lived thousands of years ago, and God had a special plan for him. God had chosen him to be a prophet, someone who shared messages from God to his people. So, when God appeared to Isaiah and asked him to go and share his news with the people, Isaiah had a choice to make.

Would he listen to God's voice and go to the people God was sending him to? Or would he keep living life as normal?

Isaiah made a decision to go where God was sending him. He told God he would preach his word and follow him no matter where he ended up. God used Isaiah in a super incredible way, and he can use you, too!

Fear Buster

Thinking about God calling us to preach or share his message with people can be scary! Thankfully, we can trust that no matter what God asks us to do, he will be with us every step of the way.

I AM WILLING TO GO WHERE JESUS SENDS ME

WEEK 47
DAY 2

Try This!

The story of God calling Isaiah is amazing! The creatures Isaiah sees in his dream where God calls him are very unique. Read Isaiah 6:1-8 and draw pictures of what's happening in the space on the right.

It was in the year King Uzziah died that I saw the Lord. He was sitting on a lofty throne, and the train of his robe filled the Temple. Attending him were mighty seraphim, each having six wings. With two wings they covered their faces, with two they covered their feet, and with two they flew. They were calling out to each other,

"Holy, holy, holy is the Lord of Heaven's Armies! The whole Earth is filled with his glory!"

Their voices shook the Temple to its foundations, and the entire building was filled with smoke.

Then I said, "It's all over! I am doomed, for I am a sinful man. I have filthy lips, and I live among a people with filthy lips. Yet I have seen the King, the Lord of Heaven's Armies."

Then one of the seraphim flew to me with a burning coal he had taken from the altar with a pair of tongs. He touched my lips with it and said, "See, this coal has touched your lips. Now your guilt is removed, and your sins are forgiven."

Then I heard the Lord asking, "Whom should I send as a messenger to this people? Who will go for us?"

I said, "Here I am. Send me."

I AM WILLING TO GO WHERE JESUS SENDS ME

Try This!

Isaiah had a dream that God called him! Use your imagination, and on this smartphone, write a conversation you and God might have if he called you.

I AM WILLING TO GO WHERE JESUS SENDS ME

WEEK 47
DAY 4

Go into all the world and preach the Good News to everyone.
Mark 16:15

Read This!

Raina and her family had lived in Zimbabwe for three years. Her mom worked at an orphanage, and her dad worked at a Bible college. Even though it was far from home, Raina knew God wanted her family to be there.

Jahcoi and his family lived on one of the poorest streets in their city. Every weekend, they volunteered at the soup kitchen. Sometimes, he would give up his room for people to stay for a few nights while they were looking for somewhere to live. Even though sometimes it was scary, he knew this is where God asked his family to be.

Pastor Taylor preached every Sunday in a small church. Even though it wasn't as exciting as what some of his friends were doing, he knew that he was doing what God asked.

God called Raina, Jahcoi, and Pastor Taylor to different places. Sometimes, God calls people to the other side of the world. Sometimes, he calls them to another place in the city, and sometimes, he wants us to share his love right where we are. The important thing is that no matter where he calls us, we are willing to go!

Prayer Prompt

Ask God to help you listen to his voice. Be willing to go wherever he calls you and your family!

WEEK 47
DAY 5

I AM WILLING TO GO WHERE JESUS SENDS ME

Try This!

Research missionaries in a country that interests you. You might know some from your church. Write down some facts about them on the lines below. If you're stuck, check your church's website for information.

Name: ______________________________

Country: ______________________________

How long they've been there: ______________________________

Do they have kids? ______________________________

What work do they do there?

____

____

____

____

How do they serve Jesus where they are?

____

____

____

____

____

Try This!

One of the ways you can show Jesus' love is to pray for people who are following God in other parts of the world. Find a world map online or in a book. Choose a country you don't know much about. Then, pray for the people who follow Jesus there. Write your prayers on the globe below.

WEEK 48
DAY 1

JESUS IS WITH ME WHEREVER I GO

> *I can never escape from your Spirit! I can never get away from your presence!*
> Psalm 139:7

Read This!

Sometimes, Kathleen felt alone. Since moving to Ontario, she didn't know very many people. She felt like she could miss school and nobody would even notice she was gone!

There were times she felt like nobody noticed her at home either. With her baby brother not sleeping much, and her older sister getting in trouble at school, she felt practically invisible.

Many nights, Kathleen would lie in bed and ask, "Does anybody notice me? Does anyone know where I am?" She was so lonely!

One night, Kathleen decided to open her Bible. She turned to the book of Psalms and started reading the words of Psalm 139.

As she read, she learned that there was nowhere she could go that God wasn't with her. He knew where she was, what she was doing, and what the future would hold. Even if nobody else noticed what was happening in her life, he did.

Just like Kathleen, there might be times when you feel alone and invisible. Remember that no matter where you are or what is happening in your life, God is right there with you!

Fear Buster

It's scary when we feel invisible or alone in life! Thankfully, we can defeat fear by remembering that there is nowhere in our lives that God doesn't see us!

JESUS IS WITH ME WHEREVER I GO

WEEK 48
DAY 2

Try This!

Describe a time in your life when you felt invisible. Then, think about if that situation happened again, what could you do differently so that you don't feel alone?

WEEK 48
DAY 3

JESUS IS WITH ME WHEREVER I GO

Try This!

Psalm 139 describes the fact that wherever we are or wherever we go, God is with us. Decorate this page with the words from Psalm 139. Include symbols, designs, fancy letters, and drawings.

I can never escape from your Spirit! I can never get away from your presence!

JESUS IS WITH ME WHEREVER I GO

WEEK 48
DAY 4

Nothing in all creation will ever be able to separate us from the love of God that is revealed in Christ Jesus our Lord.

Romans 8:39

Read This!

What is the furthest place you've ever traveled? Maybe you've been on a road trip with your family to another state or flown on a plane to another country.

How was it different than your home? Depending on where you went, the weather was probably different. You might have eaten different foods or tried new things.

Our world is so big and so diverse! You could travel for months and never see all of it. Every place you go has different customs, culture, and food.

Even though our world is humongous, God sees every single part of it! His presence is everywhere. No matter if you're sitting in your room at home or sitting on an airplane halfway across the world, God is right there with you.

The Bible tells us that no matter where we go, or even what we do, God's love will go with us! Nothing can keep us away from him. That is one super incredible promise. We can do anything and go anywhere when God is on our side!

Prayer Prompt

Thank God for his presence no matter where you are!

WEEK 48
DAY 5

JESUS IS WITH ME WHEREVER I GO

Try This!

What is the coolest trip you've ever been on with your family? It might have been a journey across the world or a trip to the next town over. Write a journal entry to describe that trip. At the end, say a quick prayer thanking God that he was with you while you were there!

JESUS IS WITH ME WHEREVER I GO

WEEK 48
DAY 6

Try This!

Use this sign language code in the box to the right to discover the words! Hint: the signs in the code are in alphabetical order, and each sign represents a letter of the alphabet!

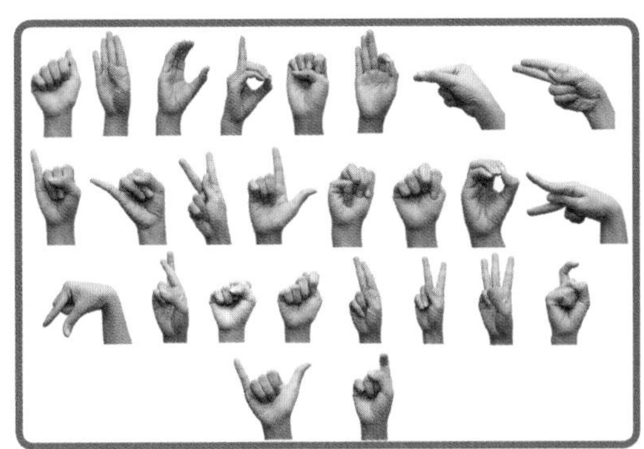

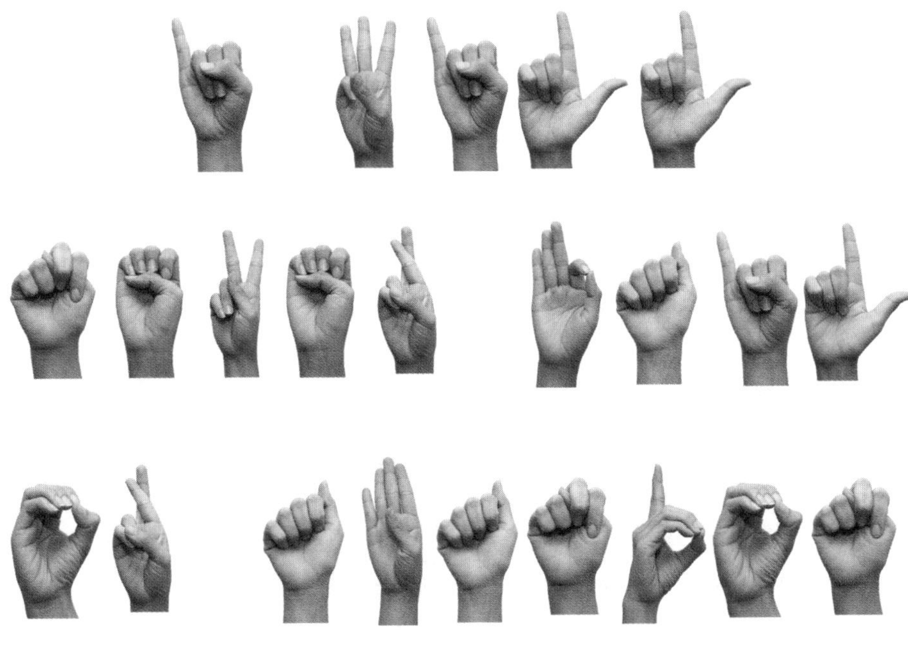

Answers on Page 319

WEEK 49
DAY 1

GOD HAS A PLAN FOR MY LIFE RIGHT NOW

I knew you before I formed you in your mother's womb. Before you were born I set you apart.

Jeremiah 1:5

Read This!

Ryder loved the art classes he'd been taking after school. When he held a paintbrush, markers, or even clay, it felt like he was coming alive! He could hardly describe how excited he felt when he got a chance to make art.

And, he was really good at it. His teacher, his friends, and his mom said so.

What Ryder especially loved was using art to show others God's love! At church, he'd been able to help out with the mural they were painting in the nursery. Even though his part was small, he was still painting something! He'd also started making birthday cards for the other kids in his small group. He loved drawing a special design for each of them.

God gave Ryder a special talent for art, and he was using it! Even as a kid, Ryder could use his art to show other's God's love. What things do you love? What talents has God given you? Whatever they are, you can use them for God's special purpose!

Fear Buster

Using our talents in front of others can be scary. What if they don't like them? We can be confident that no matter what others say, God loves it when we use our talents for him!

GOD HAS A PLAN FOR MY LIFE RIGHT NOW

WEEK 49
DAY 2

Try This!

It's time for a talent show! Grab some friends or family members, and get everyone to contribute one talent to the show. If their talent requires some prep beforehand (drawing, painting, building), give them some advanced warning! Make some plans for your talent show on this page.

WEEK 49
DAY 3

GOD HAS A PLAN FOR MY LIFE RIGHT NOW

Try This!

Art provides so many ways for you to express your talent for God! Find some art supplies—paint, markers, pencils, crayons, or anything else you can think of—and create a masterpiece for God! You might not feel like a talented artist like Ryder, but God loves the work you do!

GOD HAS A PLAN FOR MY LIFE RIGHT NOW

WEEK 49
DAY 4

Every day of my life was recorded in your book. Every moment was laid out before a single day had passed.
Psalm 139:16

Read This!

If you had twenty-four hours to do whatever you wanted, what would you do?

There are so many options! You could spend the day playing with friends, visiting a shopping mall or park, or just hanging out with your family. Maybe you'd like to visit someone you love, play a sport you're great at, or just sit down and read a book.

All of us would spend those hours differently! That's because God made all of us different. Each of us loves different things. No matter what things we love to do, or what we're good at, we can all use our days to live for God.

If you love playing sports, you can play your very best to bring God glory! You can share his love with the others on your team.

If you love music, you can sing and play songs that worship Jesus.

If you're into baking or cooking, you can show other people God's love by making them something special.

How can you use what you love for God's purpose today?

Prayer Prompt

Ask God to help you use your life for his plan and purpose!

GOD HAS A PLAN FOR MY LIFE RIGHT NOW

Try This!

The greatest purpose for your life is to show God's love to others! Inside this giant heart, brainstorm as many ways as possible to show God's love to the people around you.

GOD HAS A PLAN FOR MY LIFE RIGHT NOW

WEEK 49
DAY 6

Try This!

What are some of the things you love to do? Here are some ideas of talents and gifts that people have. Circle the ones that you love the most or you're the best at! After you're done, think of some ways you could use those things for God!

SINGING

TAKING CARE OF OTHERS

PHOTOGRAPHY

PLAYING INSTRUMENTS

PLAYING WITH LITTLE KIDS

INTERIOR DECORATING

BAKING

SERVING

GARDENING

COOKING

CLEANING

THINKING

PLAYING SPORTS

ORGANIZING THINGS

SCIENCE

RUNNING

PUBLIC SPEAKING

MATH

MAKING CRAFTS

MAKING FRIENDS

MAKING MOVIES

PAINTING

SPENDING TIME WITH FAMILY

REMEMBERING FACTS

DRAWING

READING

PLAYING GAMES

USING COMPUTERS

EXPLORING

WRITING

BRAINSTORMING

BUILDING

LEADING A GROUP

WOODWORKING

ACTING

TECHNOLOGY

DESIGNING CLOTHES

SPORTS

HELPING ANIMALS

WEEK 50
DAY 1

GOD HAS A PLAN FOR MY FUTURE

"For I know the plans I have for you," declares the LORD, "They are plans for good and not for disaster, to give you a future and a hope."

Jeremiah 29:11

Read This!

Even though Traci was only in grade six, she was already thinking about what she might study in college.

There were so many options. She could be a doctor like her Aunt Leanne, a teacher like her best friend's mom, or even a construction worker like her dad.

When she thought about all the things she could be and the careers she could choose, it felt overwhelming! How would she ever know what the right thing for her was to do?

One day after church, Traci stayed behind to talk to her children's pastor about how she was feeling. Pastor Kim pointed Traci to a verse in the Bible, where God explains he has a plan for our lives! The plan he has is good. He will take care of us.

Pastor Kim told Traci that as long as she kept following God, and living for him, he would work out his super incredible plan for her life. When the time came for her to decide what to study in college, he would help her!

Traci felt relieved! Her future was in God's hands, not just her own. He had a super incredible plan for her life, and she couldn't wait to see what it was.

Fear Buster

Thinking about the future can be scary! Thankfully, God has it all under control.

GOD HAS A PLAN FOR MY FUTURE

WEEK 50
DAY 2

Try This!

Draw a picture of what you think you might look like when you get older. Include what you might wear for the job you might have or the tools you might need to do it!

WEEK 50
DAY 3

GOD HAS A PLAN FOR MY FUTURE

Try This!

Think about a job you would like to have when you get older. Look up some information about that job. Then, write a short story called "The Day in the Life of a ________" Ask God to help you trust him with whatever job you might have when you get older.

GOD HAS A PLAN FOR MY FUTURE

WEEK 50
DAY 4

Lord, where do I put my hope? My only hope is in you.

Psalm 39:7

Read This!

"What's up with you?" Sam asked his brother, Luke. Luke was slumped on the couch, scrolling on his phone.

"Have you read the news lately?" Luke asked without making eye contact.

"Nope," said Sam as he pulled a bag of chips from the snack drawer. "It's always depressing."

Luke sighed and put down his phone. "I don't know why I read it. My teacher from my Current Events class said that we should stay informed, but it just freaks me out. It feels like the world is falling apart."

The world we live in can be pretty scary. If you ever watch the news or even hear people talking, you may see and hear some confusing and scary things. It can make you feel like running away and hiding!

Hearing about what's going on in the world may make you ask a lot of questions about the future. What kind of jobs will there be? What will our country be like? What will my family do? Where will I live?

All of us ask these kinds of questions sometimes. It's normal to be scared and have questions about the future. Thankfully, the Bible tells us that when we have questions about what lies ahead, there's one person we can always count on—God!

We can have hope that no matter what the future holds, God will be with us! When we have questions or are feeling confused about God's plan for our lives, we can talk to him. He is the hope for our future and the future of the world!

Prayer Prompt

Tell God some of the questions you have about your future. Ask him to give you peace!

WEEK 50
DAY 5

GOD HAS A PLAN FOR MY FUTURE

Try This!

What do you think life will be like in fifty years? Draw some pictures of what you think the world will look like! What kind of vehicles will we drive? What kind of food will we eat? What will our houses look like? What kind of technology will we use?

GOD HAS A PLAN FOR MY FUTURE

WEEK 50
DAY 6

Try This!

The future can be confusing and scary sometimes! Decode this confusing message to find the truth about the future!

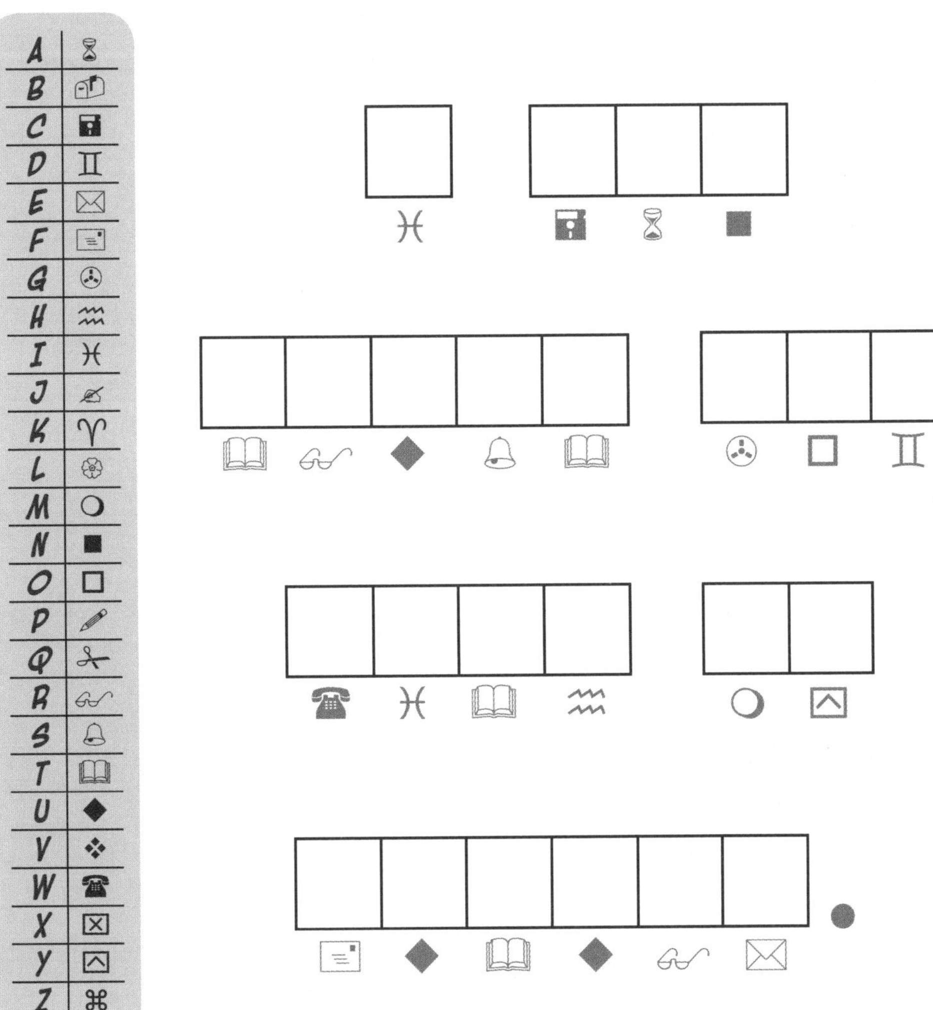

Answers on Page 319

WEEK 51
DAY 1

GOD CAN USE MY LIFE IN SUPER INCREDIBLE WAYS

I will guide you along the best pathway for your life. I will advise you and watch over you.

Psalm 32:8

Read This!

Jonathan turned the map sideways. Beside him, his sixteen-year-old sister, Malia was driving the car. "Right or left?" she asked as they approached the intersection. Jonathan turned the map again.

"Right or left?" Malia's voice rose.

"I'm not sure," Jonathan admitted, "My phone just died and I'm not sure where we are on this map!"

Have you ever had to use a map? It can be tricky! If you don't know how to use the map correctly, it can be pretty easy to get lost. Thankfully, in today's world, you can find a map with the click of a button on your computer or phone.

No matter if it's on paper or on your phone, we all need maps when we're heading to new places. Without them, we'll get lost and not know where we're going.

The same is true when we're trying to figure out where we should go or what we should do in life. We need someone to guide us and direct us.

God promises that he will direct our lives if we follow him. He has a super incredible plan for every day of our lives if we're willing to ask him, trust him and follow him!

Fear Buster

God has a great big plan for our lives! We don't need to be scared of what the future holds when we ask him to direct us.

Try This!

Are you good at directions? Test your knowledge by writing directions from your house to your school, church, or other familiar location. Be as specific as possible—include road names, building names, and specific turns. Once you're finished, ask an adult to check your directions!

Try This!

One of the ways we can hear God's direction for our lives is to pray! On this page, write a prayer to God asking him for help and direction. You can ask for help in situations right now or things that will come in the future!

GOD CAN USE MY LIFE IN SUPER INCREDIBLE WAYS

WEEK 51
DAY 4

In the same way, let your good deeds shine out for all to see, so that everyone will praise your Heavenly Father.
Matthew 5:16

Read This!

Christina is a police officer in Boston. She prays every day on her way to work and asks God to protect her fellow police officers. She always tries to show the love of Jesus to the people she meets, even the ones who are breaking the law!

Roxana is a chef at a restaurant in Mexico. As she prepares meals for the people who come in to find a seat, she says a prayer asking God to bless them. A few weeks ago, she got a chance to tell one of the waitresses the story of Jesus!

Max is a teacher at a small school in Alberta. He gets to share the love of Jesus with his students every day by being kind, giving them a smile, and loving them no matter what.

Although their lives are all different, each of these people is living out God's plan for them! They are showing the love of Jesus to the people who cross their paths.

No matter what job you end up having or where you end up living, God's greatest plan for your life is for you to show God's love to the people you meet! What a super incredible plan!

Prayer Prompt

Ask God to help you shine his light and show his love for all the days of your life.

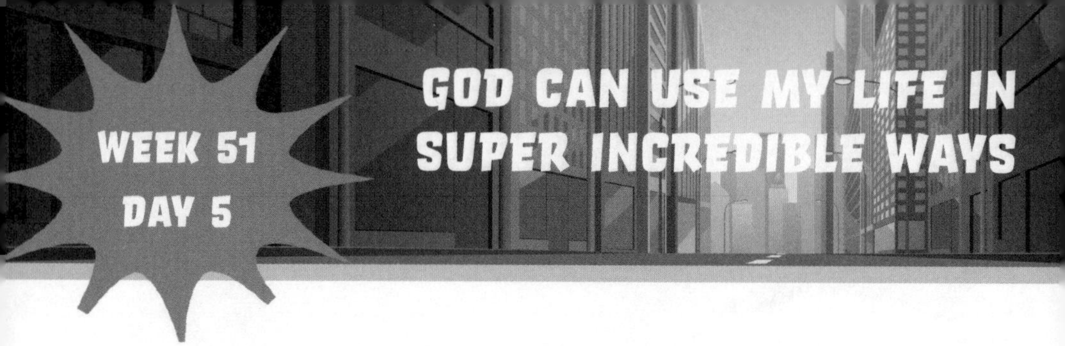

WEEK 51 DAY 5

GOD CAN USE MY LIFE IN SUPER INCREDIBLE WAYS

Try This!

Christina, Roxana, and Max show the light of Jesus through their jobs. You don't have to be an adult working at a job to show his light, though. You can shine in everything you do. Draw some examples of how you can shine Jesus' light in your everyday life in the boxes below.